MAKING BIRDHOUSES & FEEDERS

MAKING BIRDHOUSES & FEEDERS

Charles R. Self

S Sterling Publishing Co., Inc.   New York

Library of Congress Cataloging in Publication Data
Self, Charles R.
    Making birdhouses & feeders.

    Includes index.
    1. Birdhouses—Design and construction.
2. Bird feeders—Design and construction.
I. Title. II. Title: Making birdhouses and feeders.
QL676.5.S37   1985   690′.89   85-8654
ISBN 0-8069-5750-6
ISBN 0-8069-6244-5 (pbk.)

Published by Sterling Publishing Co., Inc.
Two Park Avenue, New York, N.Y. 10016
Distributed in Australia by Capricorn Book Co. Pty. Ltd.
Unit 5C1 Lincoln St., Lane Cove, N.S.W. 2066
Distributed in the United Kingdom by Blandford Press
Link House, West Street, Poole, Dorset BH15 1LL, England
Distributed in Canada by Oak Tree Press Ltd.
℅ Canadian Manda Group, P.O. Box 920, Station U
Toronto, Ontario, Canada M8Z 5P9

Contents

Acknowledgments

With thanks to fellow members of the National Association of Home and Workshop Writers who have helped me stay afloat long enough to work on this book, and, as always, to my wife, Caroline, who always helps me hold my temper with machines that don't work as I wish them to.

Introduction

The construction of birdhouses and bird feeders can be as simple or as complex as you wish to make it. When I began the first draft of this book, I was using only power tools to produce birdhouses for the book's photographs, but since then I have been burned out of my house and have had to reproduce almost every project. As a result, I was forced for a short time to use nothing other than hand tools. I switched as quickly as I could, of course, to power tools, but if nothing else, by using hand tools so recently I feel confident when I say a project is buildable with only hand tools. There's not much room for speculation, since for a while, that's the only way I could build anything.

Birdhouses and nesting boxes need no ornamentation to serve the birds using them, but an attractive design can enhance a yard or house. I have included a number of options here. Of greater importance to the birds is the correct size and placement of the entry hole, and the size of the nest floor and overall box. A birdhouse for small birds also serves as protection from larger birds and from many predators who are unable to enter through the small hole. Other defenses are often needed against other animals, and those are discussed in later chapters.

Bird feeders in a wide variety of styles and sizes can serve to fill up your yard with birds. You may not always like the species that visit, but you'll certainly get birds! Changing feed types can help determine which types of birds arrive.

Wooden bird baths are relatively easy to make. The most frequent mistake made when building them seems to be in adding too much depth, which can endanger the birds. Depths will be examined, but in general no bird bath needs to be more than 2 inches deep, and 1½ inches is preferable.

Construction techniques for birdhouses don't require any particular type of material. It is best to use wood as it comes from the dealer; no planing is necessary. If you live in a cold climate, you'll want to use thick boards for better insulation. Birds need to conserve body heat and to be protected from too much heat. Wood is a much better insulator than some may think. When possible use boards that are a full ¾ inch thick. In mild climates use lightweight wood—just heavy enough to contain the construction. It will save you money and may save work. Some wood species in boards less than ⅜ inch thick, however, may be difficult to nail, glue, or otherwise join securely.

The chapters on bird feed and bird species are not very technical. Although I enjoy birds, their feeding and housing, I don't care to retain the ornithologist's list of Latin names; my wife, the biologist and bird expert in the family, will sit still for only so long as I question and type. I get as big a kick out of a few flickers in the yard as I do from seeing the shier pileated woodpecker in the nearby woods. In fact, if I'm rushed, I sometimes confuse the two.

The major emphasis, however, will be on birdhouse and bird-feeder design and construction. You may wish to make some for sale or simply to make a few for your own and friends' yards. The instructions and drawings strive for clarity and simplicity to make the work as easy as possible with the most attractive results possible. I hope you enjoy the woodworking, and later, caring for and feeding the birds.

1
CHOOSING WOOD MATERIALS

Choosing Wood Materials

When you first look at the prices of ready-made birdhouses and bird feeders, you may wonder how economical it will be to build your own. What should quickly become clear is that whoever is producing those units is making a profit, or hoping to, and that their materials, tool set-up, and other costs are all amortized in the retail price along with mark ups for the manufacturer's and retailer's profit. Also included may be a distributor's profit. Thus you must be able to produce them more cheaply, particularly if woodworking is a hobby you enjoy and most required tools are on hand or can be used later for other jobs. In addition, if you plan to make only one or two types you're almost certain to have on hand enough scrap material from another project so that the materials end up costing almost nothing.

And quality is another consideration. You can make your birdhouses to a standard almost no manufacturer can afford to meet. Instead of galvanized brads, you might want to use brass wood screws, properly inserted into drilled and countersunk pilot holes, for example. But few are needed, so the cost is minimal. Birdhouses and bird feeders need not be of top woodworking quality, however. In most cases you won't want to waste a lot of good varnish and lacquer on them.

The woods you choose may be exotic, in those instances where such wood would lend attractiveness or a unique quality to the overall design, or like most people you could zip along with plain old pine or scraps of exterior-grade plywood.

Wood is one of the finest materials to work with. It is strong, flexible, durable, easy to work, has good insulating qualities, and is an attractive substance whether finished or unfinished. It can be shaped by the beginner with some ease and by experienced workers with greater and greater ease.

A list of domestic woods I consider suitable for building birdhouses is in Appendix A (page 120), where you will note that some wood species grow in areas not officially recognized. I've cut hickory, for example, through southern Virginia and into the lower portions of upstate New York, so I know it is there, though my reference books disagree. Some woods, like walnut, are unsuitable for birdhouses and bird feeders because of cost. So walnut's not listed, while others are just hard to locate in any but the smallest bits and pieces (beech is plain *hard* to find anywhere I've been in recent years). There's no reason why you can't use such wood if you have scraps on hand. The list is meant to be suggestive, not definitive.

In general, the pines will almost always be the material of choice, whether as solid woods or as plywoods. Firs and spruces are close behind, and the nearest to ideal wood, except for cost, is redwood. Actually, redwood's high price may be deceptive if you consider its superb durability. No finish is needed, and the wood weathers to an attractive silver grey. The resulting birdhouse or bird feeder is likely to outlast the builder. Because of redwood's near ideal qualities, I will cover its features, availability, and cost later in this chapter.

Solid woods are usually easiest to handle when constructing birdhouses and bird feeders, but in some cases plywoods, a good second choice, or wafer board (slices of wood that have been bonded together) might be more economical or handier. Always use exterior-grade plywood. I've found that a grade B face is best for exposed exterior work. It may not be perfect, but it might save you several dollars per panel over the grade A, depending on panel thickness and general specifications.

Plywood Styles

Plywood comes in so many face patterns that deciding which one to use for a specific project is very difficult. In general, the cheapest face grades are those that offer touch-sanded or unsanded fir or pine veneers, in grades A or B. Grade C is cheaper yet, but cannot be patched well. The primary difference between grades A and B, according to the American Plywood Association, is in allowable defects. Grade B is allowed minor sanding and patching defects not to exceed 5 percent of the panel's face area; discolorations not found in grade A are also allowed.

Another face grade for construction plywood is grade N, which should be used when a clear finish is desired. Boards of grade N must be made totally from heartwood or sapwood in each classified face, and there cannot be more than two pieces in a 48-inch-wide panel. Grain and color matches must be good, and only small patches are allowed (the smaller the allowable patch for a grade, the smaller the allowable defect). Grade N is much more expensive than grade A and not all lumberyards carry it. Generally, grade C is allowed larger knots (up to 1½ inches across the grain, which is usually the smallest dimension for a knot), open defects, and

sanding defects that do not impair the strength of the panel. It tends to be plenty strong but rough looking.

Usually grades C and D are classified in interior ply grades where appearance matters little, but grade C is frequently used as sheathing plywood as well and is available in exterior grades. Grade C may be economical, but if the product is to have a visible finish, you'll have to apply a lot of wood filler. If you're not looking for the ultimate finish, C-plugged plywood is suitable for most bird houses and feeders.

Choose plywood that is thick enough to insulate the finished birdhouse (feeders don't need insulation) and to hold wood screws or nails. Avoid plywoods under ⅜ inch thick, and you'll be fine. For all purposes but insulation, I think that ½-inch-thick plywood for birdhouses and bird feeders is an optimum size. Thus, if you make the floor and walls of a birdhouse with ½-inch plywood and the roof with ¾-inch-thick plywood, then all is well. On the other hand, you may find that a lighter-weight wood will produce a more attractive line in various parts of a birdhouse, making the overall construction more graceful looking. The actual difference in insulating quality is small and may be improved in other ways, for example by adding ½-inch-thick Styrofoam (expanded polystyrene) or other plastic foam to the inside of a birdhouse roof before final assembly.

Various types of plywood are meant for siding use, including such types as Texture 1–11, which is made with grooves running vertically at 8-inch intervals. These are well suited for birdhouse construction. Most are available in ½-inch and ⅝-thicknesses. There is a wide variety of surface textures and designs. You might ask a construction boss if he thinks any small pieces will be left after his crew finishes a building. Ask once when the job is beginning and remind him later on if the original answer was yes.

Redwood

A close to ideal product, redwood in its natural state is just as durable as pressure-treated wood and is nontoxic, which makes it appropriate for both bird houses and feeders (Illus. 1). Pressure-treated wood is not listed as safe) for contact with human foods, so you should

Illus. 1. This redwood flicker house uses 1½-inch × No. 6 flathead brass wood screws. The six that were used to attach the front piece can be quickly removed to facilitate cleaning.

be very careful about using it where it comes into contact with food for animals. The danger may be minimal, but there's little sense in taking any chances, even though the cost is probably two thirds that of redwood. Since the amount of lumber used is so small for most birdhouses and bird feeders, you probably won't save more than a buck. Redwood and the cedars may cause allergic skin reactions in some people. As with pressure-treated woods, cut redwood and cedar while wearing a good quality dust mask and do not allow sawdust or sanding dust to remain on your skin for long periods of time. Wash separately all clothing worn during work.

Recently I picked up some Clear All Heart redwood for 30 percent less per board foot (a board foot is one square foot of wood, one

inch thick, nominally) than usual. The price was so reasonable probably because it was from a distress sale carload lot. In any case, you need *not* get Clear All Heart redwood to build birdhouses. It may be the most durable grade and, to many people the most attractive with its even grain pattern, but it's also the most expensive. I got it because it was easy to find, but it is usually difficult to come by in the East and particularly in certain areas of the Southeast.

Properties. Redwood's properties include a very fine-looking grain and color, which weathers nicely to silver grey over time. The fresh milled color ranges from brownish pink to cinnamon brown in the heartwood, and the sapwood is cream colored. The heartwood's durability is almost legendary, with a built-in resistance to decay and insects, which makes it ideal for products that are to be placed on or close to the ground. The sapwood, however, is *not* any more resistant than any other softwood.

Redwood is pliable and very lightweight. Its straight grain with fine texture and its low level of contained pitch and resins make it a rival of white pine, which is considered by most to be the easiest to shape.

Finish is no problem with redwood. If you wish, you can apply a clear finish, but it's not necessary. Because of redwood's durability, very high resistance to checking, and good dimensional stability, it doesn't really need a finish.

Grades. When selecting redwood, consider the number of grades suitable for birdhouse and bird-feeder construction. Clear All Heart is best for posts and is the most attractive. Otherwise, the so-called garden grades are perfectly suitable for virtually every use. In fact, Construction Heart, one of the garden grades, is also suitable for use in-ground, as is Merchantable Heart.

Construction Heart redwood has knots, blemishes, and manufacturing imperfections, but it is decay resistant. Use it for posts, feeder and birdhouse floors, and where moisture or insects might cause problems.

Construction Common is similar to Construction Heart but contains sapwood, making it less durable when on or near the ground. I prefer the textural and color changes of sapwood.

Merchantable Heart is another All Heartwood grade. Its defects include some loose knots and a few knotholes. It is ideal for the lightweight structural support necessary for birdhouses and bird feeders, and it is far cheaper than other All Heart grades.

Merchantable contains larger knots and more imperfections than Construction Common grade, with loose knots and some knotholes. If it's readily available in your area, try it for small projects. You'll often find that cutting around defects is easy, and you will save a few dollars as well.

Availability. Redwood is not consistently available in all grades nationwide. In my area so little of it is requested that one major distributor is thinking of discontinuing the line. (He might, however, reconsider if he knew that the reason I didn't buy from him, or one of his preferred retailers, recently, was because they didn't have the sizes I desired.) In general, though, redwood can be easily and quickly ordered by any lumberyard or building supply dealer. Obviously, large orders are likely to get more attention than small ones, but in general, lumberyards are among the few remaining businesses that go the extra step for a customer.

Finding woods Perhaps a note is needed here on locating certain species of woods for constructing birdhouses and bird feeders. When I state that a wood is hard to find, I don't mean it can't be found. The point is that you will have to try a half dozen or so lumberyards, place an order, or make a trip to a specialty house. Hard-to-locate woods involve that sort of extra time and effort. In most cases, I can locate any wood generally available in my hemisphere by going to every lumber supplier within 25 miles of my house. But that's not a trip I want to make when I need only 6 board feet of wood to build a feeder!

Pine, fir, and some redwood can all be found at nearly any lumberyard, and in some areas cedar is readily available, too. All you have to do is decide what you want and ask for it.

2
CONSTRUCTION MATERIALS

Construction Materials

Although wood is the primary material used to construct birdhouses and bird feeders, you will also need fasteners of various kinds, perhaps a bit of sheet metal, and sometimes poles made of material other than wood. These requirements are not very expensive but can make a large and long-term difference in how much durability and comfort your bird house or feeder provides.

Nails

Today, nails are the most common fasteners for wood and for good reason. Properly selected and applied, nails make secure, cheap fasteners that are as durable as almost any other. Proper selection of nails is very important. Most people are not aware that a wide variety of nails is available from most lumberyards.

For lightweight wood constructions that are to be used outdoors, use weatherproof nails and screws. If you choose mild (soft) steel nails, then use only hot-dipped galvanized ones. Otherwise, use aluminum nails. My only objection to aluminum nails is that they bend too easily if hit at a slight angle. The difference in cost between the two is minimal or nonexistent, because there are about three times as many aluminum nails per pound as steel.

In most cases 6d (six-penny) and 4d (four-penny) casing or finishing nails will be sufficient and will not be so visible that they mar your finishing job, if any. For thicker wood, use 8d nails. Annularly threaded or screw shank nails are not necessary for birdhouse or bird-feeder assembly but are good for attaching the finished unit to a pole or tree.

When attaching a piece of wood that is about 1 inch thick to a post, a good rule of thumb is to use nails three times longer than the actual wood thickness (1-inch stock is usually ¾ inch thick). Thus, a 2¼-inch-long nail is sufficient for such stock, but a shorter one is not. If you must use shorter nails, then install more than are called for, but you will obtain better results by employing the correct length. Size 4d common and finishing nails measure 1½ inches long, 6d are 2 inches long, 8d are 2½ inches long, and 10d are 3 inches long. (See Appendix B, page 122). The number of nails per pound can also be estimated. Obviously, the smaller the nail, the more you get per pound. Aluminum nails yield about three times more per pound as the chart in Appendix B shows.

Wood Screws

Selecting a wood screw for bird constructions is fairly easy. Either hot-dipped galvanized screws, which are used as you would galvanized nails, or brass screws are suitable. But aluminum screws, in my experience, don't hold up well unless you are extremely careful when drilling pilot holes and inserting the screw.

Flathead and oval-head wood screws are best for bird constructions and are readily available in the required head and shank sizes from most hardware dealers. For any project in which you need extra holding power, use a No. 6 or a No. 8 screw. Flathead screws should be 1½ times the thickness of one of the boards being joined, and round-head screws should be 1¼ times the board thickness. This provides in both instances more than enough holding power and keeps the screw head from penetrating the surface totally when you join two flat pieces of the same size. Almost always, then, you will need 1-inch or 1¼-inch flathead or oval-head screws and 1¼ inch round-head screws for 1-inch boards. Thicker boards require appropriate screw size adjustments.

Brass wood screws are slightly preferable to galvanized for overall durability. Although they are more expensive, only a small number of brass screws are required for any project in this book.

Miscellaneous Materials

Various other bits of hardware may be needed, such as bolts and nuts or hook-and-eye units, but in almost every case you can simply use the smallest size that will make the span. Make sure the hardware is galvanized to keep rust at bay.

In general, the only other materials you may need are some wire, a few sheet-metal screws, and other items for special applications. Be sure that they too are galvanized if you want them to last.

Pipe

Pipe is probably the best support you could use if you don't plan to attach the bird house or feeder to a tree. Select pipe up to 1½ inches in diameter, with fittings to match.

One fitting that you will need is a floor flange, which is attached to the pipe end and to which the bird house or feeder is then screwed. Be sure to choose a pipe brand that will accommodate a flange. If the flange is for galvanized pipe, you need pipe whose end is threaded to fit the female flange thread. If you use PVC (polyvinyl chloride) pipe, attach the fitting with solvent cement.

The choice between galvanized and PVC pipe isn't all that hard. If you've got one or the other on hand, use it. If you have to buy it, get the PVC because it costs about half of what the galvanized does, weighs less, and cuts more easily. In addition, you don't have to worry about threading. But if you make a martin house, for example, that weighs 35 pounds or so, then for more support buy galvanized piping or a 2-inch or larger PVC pipe.

In either case, the smooth exterior of PVC piping makes climbing difficult for any predatory animal, because there are no wooden surfaces for claws to dig into.

When attaching the flange to the house or feeder floor, insert screws, not nails, and select a material that will weather well. Use brass, aluminum, or galvanized screws, about 1 inch or 1¼ inch × No. 8. Most flanges take four screws, so the feeder or house should be secure against almost anything short of a tornado.

A number of other pipe products could prove handy. You might elect to make a hanging feeder that swings from an arm on the pipe instead of being attached to the top of the pipe. In that case, simply add a 90° elbow and the arm in the appropriate length of pipe. Drill the arm to accept machine bolts with formed eye heads, and wire the feeder in place.

Whatever you use to build a birdhouse or bird feeder, make sure it's weatherproof. Galvanized or noncorrosive metals last far longer than plain steel, and many plastics are almost totally impervious to weather. If noncorrosive materials, finishing nails for example, are unobtainable in your area, then cover the heads after setting the nails. Don't, however, use a wood putty, even an exterior type. Apply instead a glazier's compound, and your nonrustproof nails will last longer. The glazier's compound is usually white, and if you space the nails correctly, the white dots will look fine even in a natural-finish wood.

3
HAND
TOOLS

Hand Tools

As I've already stated, simple hand tools will suffice for building birdhouses and bird feeders. But if you want to get into mass production, then you will need power tools, such as a table saw. Still, with the wide variety of handsaws, screwdrivers, hammers, and other tools on the market these days, it pays to know which type is best for building small constructions and the quality required for lasting use. All tools are eventually mistreated in one manner or another, which af-

fects their durability and may well affect your safety. Be sure to buy top quality tools that will withstand such abuse. For house and feeder construction you will need, among other items, a claw hammer, a Phillips screwdriver, and a standard screwdriver (Illus. 2).

Hammers

Most people seem to have at least one claw hammer around. They are ideal for small

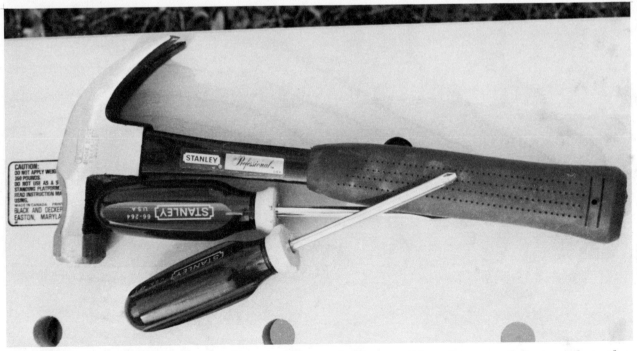

Illus. 2. These assembly tools are all you really must have to construct the projects in the following chapters: a Phillips screwdriver, a standard or cabinet-tip screwdriver, and a claw hammer.

construction purposes. If you need to buy one, get either a 13-ounce or 16-ounce hammer. I recommend the 16-ounce because it is good for general use and feels right for about 80 percent of the people who try to use a hammer. You can do any job required here quite easily without wielding a heavier hammer.

Be sure to choose a claw style and handle material suitable to you and your work. For light work, I prefer a curved-claw hammer because the curved claws provide a better grip for removing bent nails. For other work, I want a straight, or ripping, claw, no matter what the hammer weight. Generally, I use several of each style, in a variety of handle materials and brands. Choose a brand name you recognize and have confidence in. Avoid economy models as you would avoid avalanches. You only need one hammer, so buy the best you can find.

Handle material causes a slight difference in the price of a hammer. Wood is, of course, the traditional handle material and is just as good today as it was several hundred years ago and better in fact in most cases. Fibreglass is a bit more costly but to me well worth it. Fibreglass handles provide the resilence of wood in absorbing shock from nailing, while approaching the strength of a steel handle. Steel, particularly solid-steel, handles provide the least shock absorption of all—none. Tubular-steel handles provide, I believe, a better feel and at least minimal shock absorption (Illus. 3).

Both fibreglass and steel handles have a rubber or soft-plastic grip, which aids in holding the hammer when your hand gets sweaty. It also provides minimal shock absorption.

Look for a good, forged head, with cleanly cut claws and a good polish on all unpainted parts. The face will be slightly belled, or convex, and may be round or octagonal, depending on the maker. Recently I have investigated some locally made brands of hammers. Although difficult to find at my usual dealers, they have been praised by my woodworking friends. Their loyalty, I suspect, is based on the lower price.

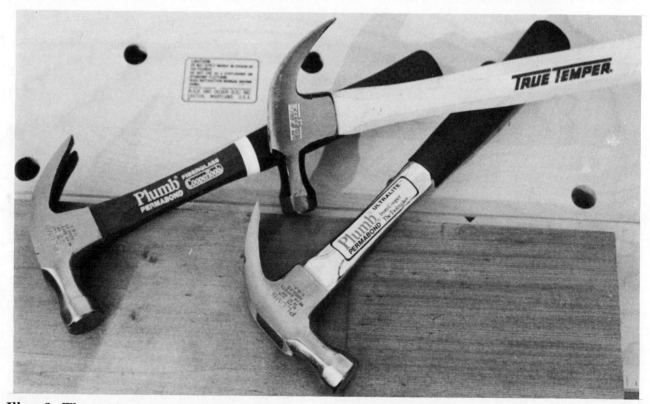

Illus. 3. Three 16-ounce curved-claw hammers that have different kinds of handles: (*left*) fibre- **glass handle, (*center*) wood handle, (*right*) tubular steel handle.**

Handsaws

Like hammers, handsaws come in a wide variety of styles and sizes. For bird buildings, the only saw you need is a crosscut handsaw. It comes in many different grades of quality, and prices vary accordingly. Although some people say that the continental European style (a bow saw) is better than a handsaw, I disagree. Select a handsaw of medium quality or better. You'll want no less than eight, and preferably ten, teeth per inch. Handsaws are generally available with up to a dozen teeth per inch, but they add more work to the cut (though the cut is smoother) (Illus. 4, 5).

Illus. 4. Fine-tooth (12 teeth per inch) handsaw is an excellent saw for finishing or general purposes.

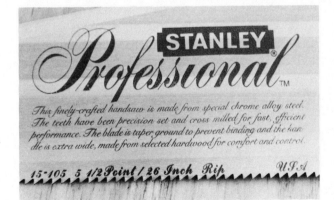

Illus. 5. A rip saw offers 5½ teeth per inch.

One good reason for selecting top quality hand tools is that they save you energy. First, they are better designed to fit your hands and their movements, so the work will go more easily (Illus. 6). Second, if edged, they stay sharp much longer, reducing time and cost for sharpening. Third, you won't end up

flinging them across the room, with steam spurting from your ears, when you realize the five-dollar special will *never* cut a straight line.

Illus. 6. This handsaw is being used to complete a cut that was begun with a circular saw, which would have made the cut too deep on one of the boards if used for the finish. A circular saw blade, when stopped in a cut that does not go completely through a board, leaves an arc. If you saw to a mark, the shorter edge of the arc will be inside, or short of, the mark, so you must saw past the mark to complete the cut, producing an overcut at the larger part of the arc. Thus, a handsaw is better in completing such cuts.

A coping saw is a second handy handsaw for building birdhouses, because it enables you to make circles, fancy designs, and scrollwork, to cut larger openings than your drill-bit capacities allow, or to perform several jobs that you may discover only after buying this inexpensive saw. Get one with a frame at least 6 inches high (for cutting in the center of a 1-foot-wide piece of material) and buy at least a dozen extra blades at the same time.

Drills

Styles of hand drills and drill bits are numerous, but you will need only two types: the push drill and the hand drill. Bit braces are generally reserved for heavy work.

Push drills are just what their name implies: you insert a drill point, place the point where you want to make a hole, and then push down on the drill. The point will spin and make a hole. Most such drills come with a set of points, and they provide the best and fastest means of making holes for small screws in soft wood and for brads to be placed close to edges. Drilling in such situations reduces wood splitting to almost nothing.

Hand drills enable you to use bits with chuck ends as large as ⅜ inch. These are faster than push drills, require a little less energy to make larger holes, and will readily drill holes up to ½ inch in diameter.

For larger holes, the coping saw works well or you can switch to a bit brace, which holds bits up to about 1½ inches (and adjustable bits that are even larger).

Screwdrivers

In the mistreated category, screwdrivers win all prizes, but some of those on sale won't work well for even a dozen screws. These tools, like hammers, are quite simple in most ways and don't cost a great deal individually. So it seldom makes any sense to buy a cheap one. With a high-quality screwdriver, you'll get a good steel alloy with a ground tip and a comfortable handle; work goes well, maximum torque is produced, and your forearm doesn't cramp too soon.

The handle, which can be made of any material, must be comfortable while you drive in the screws. A handle too small for your hand to hold strongly can cause slippage and be very tiring. It can also cause blisters. The quality of handle material is important; most of the best handles are made of plastic in several colors. Wood handles are also available and can be excellent. Handle shape is best determined by the individual. At least two companies have lines of screwdrivers with handles that are slightly wedge shaped—larger at the bottom where you

usually need size. I like these for heavy work, but for general or light use I prefer a straight-line design.

Tip styles must match the screws being used, which for houses and feeders are either slotted or Phillips head. The tip should fit into the screw-head slot snugly—not too wide and not too narrow. For fine work, select the style known as cabinet tip. A standard screwdriver has a flare just above the tip, but the cabinet and Phillips screwdrivers have straight blades, which enable you to turn (counter bore) screws down below the surface of the wood without tearing up the workpiece.

Squares

In addition to hand tools, you will need some measuring tools to lay out the work and to make certain that cuts are accurate and straight.

Of the many styles and shapes of squares, you will need only one of two basic kinds for these projects: a try square (Illus. 7) and a combination square (Illus. 8, 9). A try square is a solid unit with immovable handle and tongue set at a 90° angle. A combination square offers the same 90° angle but also includes a 45° marking. The handle moves along the blade so you can measure for depth quite easily. A combination square is also good for marking. It contains a scriber at the end of the square, which can be set to the proper depth and which may be moved with the square to mark the board for ripping.

Whichever square you choose, be sure to buy the best you can afford. You only need one, so check for solidity. Also check for ease of movement in a combination square. Look at the finish, as you should with all tools, and see how well the machining was done. Barring loss or theft, a try square will last a lifetime and a combination square, many years.

Measuring Tools

For working with relatively small pieces of wood, you will need a top quality, simple folding rule (Illus. 9) or a 6-foot or longer

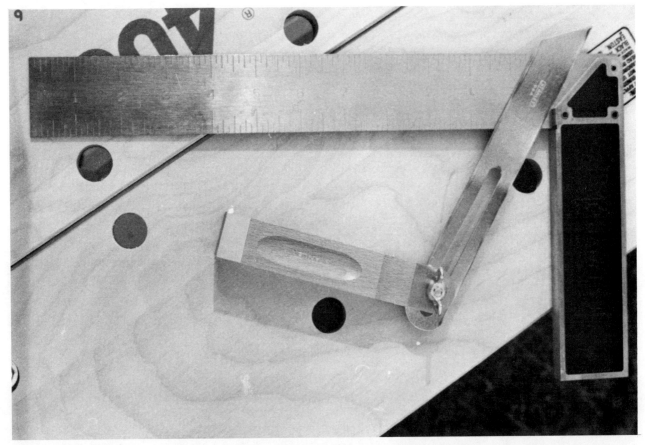

Illus. 7. Use a try square and a sliding T bevel for transferring angle measurements.

Illus. 8. Combination square.

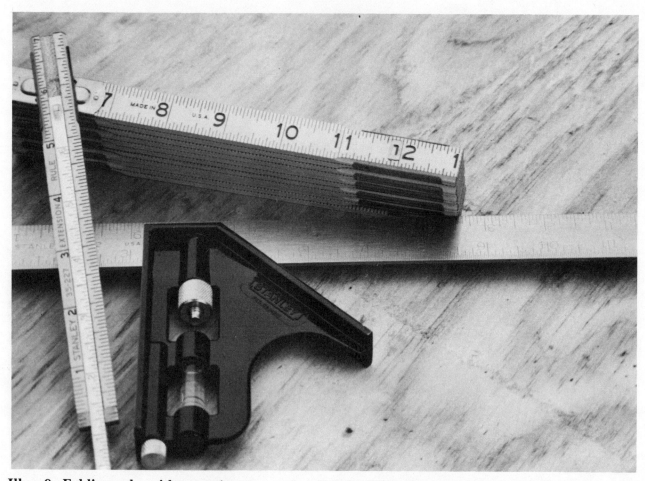

Illus. 9. Folding rule, with extension out, and a slightly different combination square.

measuring tape. You could select a straight rule 2 feet or longer and easily make do with that, though the longer ones tend to be cumbersome and hard to carry around outside a shop.

Look for clearly defined markings and ease of legibility on any measuring tool, whether rule or tape. The best folding rules are brass bound and usually have a brass inset within the first 6 inches. This can serve either to extend the overall measurement by 6 inches or to help calculate the depth of a hole (Illus. 9). Measuring tapes need a solid case and should retract easily once the locking button is pushed a second time. Locking should also be easy and secure. The wider a measuring tape is, the longer it is likely to last. Most tapes snap off in front of the 6-inch mark because of the whiplash during retraction. The shorter the tape, the less likely this is to happen, as the springs used are less powerful.

Marking Tools

Several kinds of marking tools will come in handy. The standard carpenter's pencil is flat with a large, thick lead, which lasts long, doesn't break easily, and makes sharpening easy. Whittle with a knife and sharpen with sandpaper, a stone, or any handy, rough device. Scribes leave a nearly invisible mark, which is important for finely finished work where pencil lines might be difficult to sand out (Illus. 10).

Chalk lines are important only when working with boards longer than those you would ordinarily need for houses and feeders. The shortest chalk line available is 50 feet long. Still, I use all of mine with some frequency even on relatively small pieces, since the chalk line is often easier to secure and use for marking than a straight edge and scribe.

Levels

Levelling of birdhouses and bird feeders isn't of great importance, though it's rather nice not to have them at acute angles to the ground. In most cases, a good torpedo level about 9 inches long will suffice and will also enable you to plumb any feeder or house post that you must install.

Illus. 10. To make the most accurate measurements, tip the rule or measuring tape on edge.

Mitre Boxes

Mitre boxes for building birdhouses and other small projects tend to be a problem. While they do provide a superb way of producing accurate, straight, and nearly perfectly angled cuts, the less costly models cannot cut anything wider than 4 inches, particularly when mitres are being made. Some mitre boxes can make 7-inch-wide cuts in stock at a 45° angle, but they are expensive. Other brands, though, are reasonably priced, can be used with almost any handsaw, and produce precise straight and angle cuts. The capacity of other one-wall mitre boxes can be increased by simply extending the saw size (as long as the box will accept larger saws) and providing a wider base plate. By one-wall mitre boxes, I mean those inexpensive models that have only a saw clip and a back fence.

If you select a mitre box for utility's sake you'll almost certainly choose one of the less expensive saw guides. But if you select for a lifetime of use and for other chores around the shop, you might want to consider one of the top brands of mitre boxes. In my opinion, a light-duty mitre box tends to be a waste of money because of its lack of capacity and modest durability.

The next chapter covers power tools, which are more expensive but which might prove to be convenient, not only in making birdhouses and bird feeders, but in other projects as well.

4
POWER
TOOLS

Power Tools

There are two categories of power tools: portable and stationary. Stationary tools generally offer more scope and greater accuracy, while the portable tools offer just that—portability. Some portable tools, such as the router, offer as great, or greater, scope than a stationary tool. And the common electric drill has had so many accessories developed for it that even trying to categorize its limits is difficult. Today's cordless tools offer even greater portability; power tools can now go where only hand tools were possible before.

Portable Tools

Saws. The ever-popular circular saw is in many home workshops these days for good reason. With care, you can do some amazing work with almost any of them, and an appreciation of certain types of quality will help in getting the most saw for your money.

If you're at all serious about working with wood, don't consider buying a cheap circular saw. A good consumer model saw, with a 7¼-inch blade, decent power, and durability, will cost at least 40 percent more than the cheap sale model. Look for a weighty base plate, ease of handling, ease of adjustability, and switches that match your hands well (Illus. 11).

If you're really serious about woodworking with portable tools, you might consider a professional saw. There are many brands—most are good, and some are excellent. Prices

Illus. 11. A 7¼-inch heavy-duty circular saw. This particular model is the heaviest-duty (14.5 amperes) straight-drive model I've ever seen.

begin where consumer models end. Like most portable power tools, professional models cost more, last far longer, and handle more easily—though they come with fewer fancy features—than consumer models. In the first place, professional saws have all ball and needle bearings. Case castings are more accurately machined, aligned, and assembled. The base plate is heavier, and all adjustment knobs are larger, making them easier to use for both bare and gloved hands. In almost every instance, the power cords are longer (up to 10 feet, instead of 6 feet) so that the saws can easily cut a full sheet of plywood or panelling. The cords are heavier, and most are insulated with either rubber or an expensive elastomer that stays flexible in very cold weather.

For any circular saw, choose a 7¼-inch blade. It is almost standard size, so that you'll find blades to fit in more cutting styles than with the other two popular sizes—6½-inch and 8¼-inch. There is also a 10¼-inch size available, but it's not very useful.

For most cuts with circular saws, a combination blade—but not the one that comes with the saw—is a good choice. It enables you to make reasonably smooth crosscuts, which are made across the grain, and decent rip cuts, which are made along the grain. If you do a lot of ripping, choose a rip blade since this type of cutting requires a slightly different style of blade. For extremely smooth cuts, use panel or plywood blades with large numbers of teeth and a fine set in which the teeth are not angled out as sharply from the blade.

The combination blades supplied with every circular saw I've ever had are adequate for rough framing work but not good for finer cutting. Generally, the more teeth a blade has, the finer it will cut, and you can easily find blades with as many as 200 teeth. You'll probably get the best all-around results using a planer-combination (hollow-ground–planer) blade for your work. Although the planer blade will make a rip cut, it is best at making crosscuts, which constitute about 90 percent of birdhouse and bird-feeder building (Illus. 12).

The jigsaw, or scroll saw, is a second item of interest for anyone doing much birdhouse building. These may range from inexpensive to expensive, but you don't need a professional model in this instance. Various additions are made to the basic jigsaw to produce different models. Essentially the jigsaw works by a motor drawing and pushing the blade up and down. The blades are thin so they can make scrolled cuts for fancy designs, circles, and straight cuts. Careful blade selection is important because blades designed for light, fancy, detailed scrolling work will not make good straight cuts in heavier stock. Most good jigsaws fitted with an appropriate blade will zip right through stock used for birdhouses. Buy several blades at once, since even heavier jigsaw blades have a tendency to break fairly rapidly. Fortunately this tendency is somewhat offset by their low cost.

Fancy (and more costly) jigsaws offer automatic scrolling, which enables you to keep the saw headed straight on while turning the blade with an adjustment knob, or to set it on automatic so the blade will automatically pivot as you follow the design (Illus. 13).

One such saw that is produced by Black & Decker offers an electronic feedback control. Under most conditions it will keep the speed up while the saw cuts, making for both faster and neater cutting within the saw's limits.

For coarse wood cutting choose a blade with seven t.p.i. (teeth per inch), and for fine cuts select a blade with at least ten t.p.i. Scroll-cutting blades also have ten t.p.i., and blades made for cutting very coarsely in wood may have as few as four. Metal-cutting blades range from 14 to 32 t.p.i. You can even buy a knife-edged blade to cut rubber and leather. Flush-cutting blades are shaped to enable the saw to come right up to the surface against which you're cutting, with the blade teeth extended out to the saw front.

There are a variety of other portable power saws available, but the circular saw and jigsaw will do every job you need to complete any project in this book.

Drills. The electric drill is one of the most popular home workshop tools. Many people even have more than one (Illus. 14). For light project work, there is no need to go beyond the ⅜-inch chuck size or to buy a professional drill (Illus. 15).

Look for a drill that offers a well-crafted housing, at least a two-ampere power rating,

Illus. 12. For heavy, or double, cuts a heavy-duty circular saw is the best tool. Here, two pieces of ¾-inch wafer board have been clamped for cutting. The saw blade is a 40-tooth carbide-tipped model that makes a beautifully smooth finishing cut.

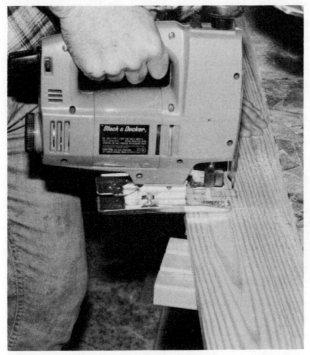

Illus. 13. Automatic scrolling jigsaws perform many complex cuts. Because they are so versatile, some people use them for all their sawing needs.

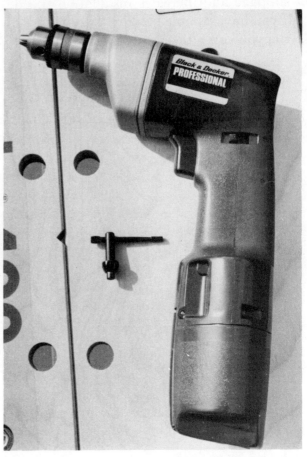

Illus. 14. Portable drills, such as this model, have improved greatly in recent years.

and a good handle for your hand (Illus. 16). The size of the chuck determines the size of the drill. Choose either the ¼-inch or ⅜-inch drill for making birdhouses and bird feeders. The latter is more versatile for household tasks, so if the prices are similar for each size, choose the larger (Illus. 16).

Electric drill accessories run the gamut from large to small and from simple to complex. See Illus. 17 and 18 for examples of a spade bit and a twist drill. You can get a variety of different drill bit types, including adjustables that extend to about 3½ inches in diameter. Screwdriver bits are available in a variety of styles. The Phillips is handier than the slotted, because there is more surface to grip. The increased use of power screwdrivers and electric drills equipped to handle such jobs is the reason for the development of many newer types of screwheads, such as Pozidriv, which offers more surface for the driver to grip and thus decreases the chances of slippage and increases installation speed.

If you have trouble holding a drill at a 90° angle, you can either buy a jig to help with

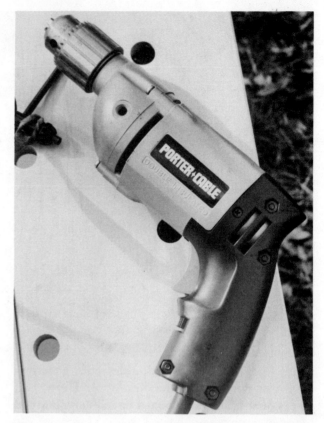

Illus. 15. Heavy-duty ⅜-inch drills are capable of many uses, and they last almost indefinitely under normal conditions.

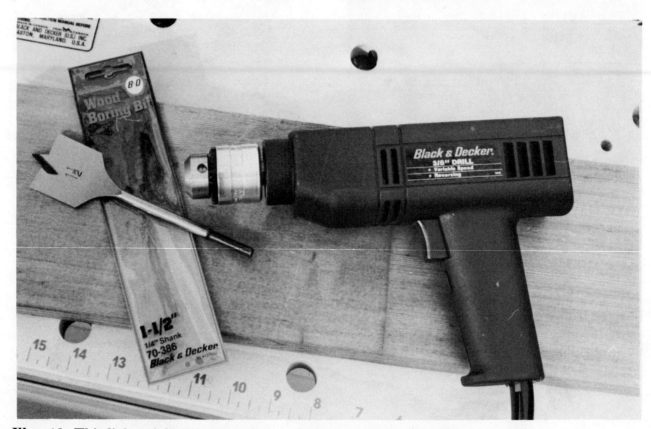

Illus. 16. This lightweight 2-ampere electric drill is very easy to handle.

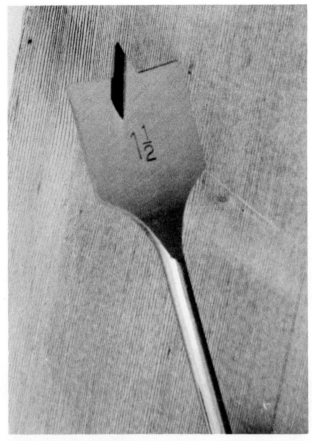

Illus. 17. Spade bit.

the job or stand a try square next to the drill while it's in use. If you want to stop holes at a particular depth, use the stops that fit right on the bit or onto the drill (a piece of duct or vinyl tape works well as a marker and is cheaper). Some drill bits, like the Forstner bit, make nearly flat-bottomed holes. They are moderately costly.

Sanders. If you use primarily stock lumber, planed at the mill, and don't expect to do a lot of jigsawing or to make long cuts on the major wood surfaces, then hand sanding is all you need for these projects. If you desire a particularly fine finish, then a pad, or finishing, sander will do the job quite well (Illus. 19).

To remove material quickly, use a belt sander. But most sanding jobs for these houses and feeders should be light enough to be done by hand or with a finishing sander. After all, a fine furniture finish isn't going to impress a bird (most actually prefer natural finishes), nor is it going to last long enough outdoors to impress anyone else.

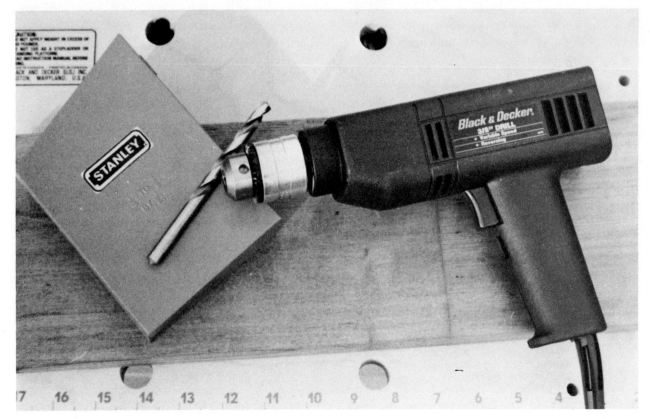

Illus. 18. Twist drills, with electric drill.

Illus. 19. A pad sander, like this professional model, is the most convenient and least expensive finishing sander to use.

Stationary Tools

The stationary power tool is the tool of accuracy. Although every project can be made with hand tools only, power and stationary tools do add speed and accuracy to the job. With table or radial saws, you can produce fine furniture, especially if you add such aids as a band saw, lathe, drill press, planer, jointer, moulder, and shaper. Such an investment is, of course, expensive and can become more so if each tool needs an individual stand and motor.

Saws. Among the stationary power tools, the saws are of greatest interest for most hobbyists, because they do more work, more quickly, and more accurately than any other type of saw or any other type of woodworking tool. Two saws are designed primarily for making straight cuts: the table saw (Illus. 20) and the radial saw. The primary difference between the two is the mounting; the table saw blade is mounted to an arbor *below* the table, while the radial saw blade is mounted to an arbor *above* the table. There are advantages and disadvantages to both. Some people find that they can make accurate cuts more easily on the radial saw because the stock stays still while the blade and motor move on a rigid arm assembly. The width of

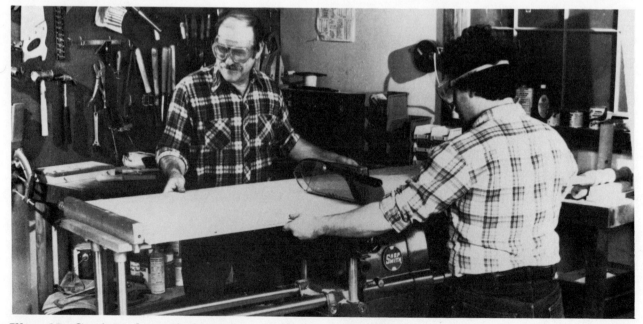

Illus. 20. Cutting plywood sheets into smaller pieces is easier with a helper, even when using a table saw and accessories. (Courtesy of Shopsmith, Inc.)

crosscuts and rip cuts on a radial saw, however, is limited to the length of that rigid arm (and the longer the arm, the less rigid it will be). But most radial saws can easily cut to the center of a 4 × 8-foot sheet of plywood. So for all practical purposes, the width of a radial saw rip is unlimited.

Certainly neither saw is essential to building birdhouses, but either can be handy and may offer features not found in other saw types. As an example, the dado blade makes dadoes (which go across the grain) and grooves (which go with the grain). These two operations would normally require two saw cuts and some work with a chisel or a lot of saw cuts to make the groove. The dado blade, however, does the job in a single pass. Most 10-inch stationary saws accept a dado unit large enough to make a slot a full ¾ inch wide and as deep as the dado blade will allow (about 2 to 3 inches for common units, though most dadoes and grooves don't require such depth). Newer table saw models take up less space than ever before, while still offering the capability to slice through a 2 × 4 at a 45° angle; blade sizes for such saws are usually 8 inches instead of the more common 10 inches.

While I tend to agree that it's nice to be able to work in a smaller space and, especially, to store a number of tools in limited space, there is a tendency on the part of toolmakers to overemphasize the space-saving aspects of such small machines, often called table- or bench-top models. As always, if you are cutting an inch off the end of a 10-foot-long board, you *must* have 10 feet of space on one side of the saw. To cut a 4 × 8-foot sheet of plywood, you still must have over 16 feet of space overall (to cut it the long way) for safe operation. I move my saw into the hallway for such operations, because my shop is only 15 feet long, and the hall is almost 24 feet long. I can cut the 1″ × 10″ × 10′ board in the shop but I can't cut the panel of plywood safely in that space.

Still, the bench models are lightweight and can be easily moved in most cases, which is more than can be said for many full-size radial and table saws, many of which weigh more than 300 pounds. Building birdhouses doesn't require much cutting of large material.

Moulding heads, another accessory for table and radial saws, may prove handy if you desire a fancy trim. A special holder fits the saw arbor, and the holder accepts knives ground in innumerable designs so you can cut moulding to any design by combining knives, or passes. On the table saw, you need not only the special head and knives, but also a different table insert with a wider slot (wider, even, than the special insert for the dado blade). Radial saws may also offer a shaper accessory, which does essentially the same job as the moulding head. Shapers can also be used on many drill presses if the presses are capable of high enough speeds. Be sure to use the full range of accessories that are designed to protect you (Illus. 21–22).

Given a choice, I don't know which of the two I'd pick—radial or table saw. Either can do an excellent job if the saw is a good one.

Band saws and jigsaws are also available. If I could have only one, I'd choose a band saw (Illus. 23). It is capable of more types of work and heavier material than the jigsaw. A stationary jigsaw (Illus. 24) is used primarily for ornamental cutting, and heavy work just causes blades to snap frequently. They're cheap and easy to change, but it is still an inconvenient task.

The woodworker's band saw, though, is an entirely different story. It can be used for mild ornamental work, though it will not come close to doing the intricate scrollwork of the jigsaw. It is extremely useful for such things as pad sawing and resawing. Pad sawing involves tacking together thin stock (up to the limit of thickness of the band-saw's cut), placing a single pattern on the top, and making a single cut or series of single cuts after which the "pad" is separated to provide exact duplicates of the pattern (Illus. 25). Resawing is nothing more than taking a board that's too thick and cutting it in halves, thirds, or quarters on the band saw (Illus. 26).

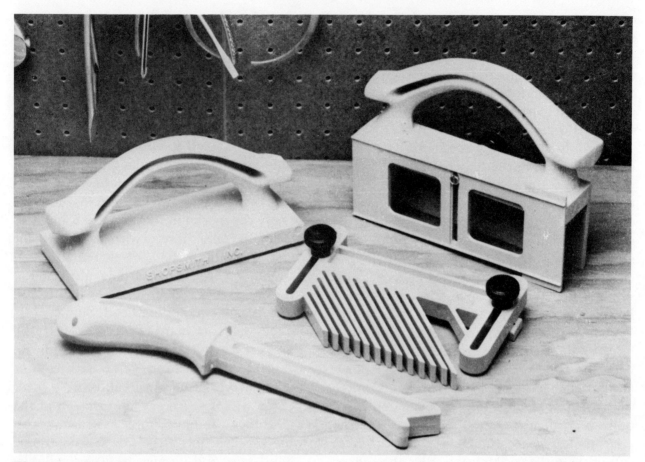

Illus. 21. The full range of saw accessories include the following: (*top left*) push block, (*left*) push stick, (*top right*) fence riding jig, (*right*) feather board. (Courtesy of Shopsmith, Inc.)

Illus. 22. Cutting bevels often requires working close to the blade, so a push stick is an essential part of your workshop. (Courtesy of Shopsmith, Inc.)

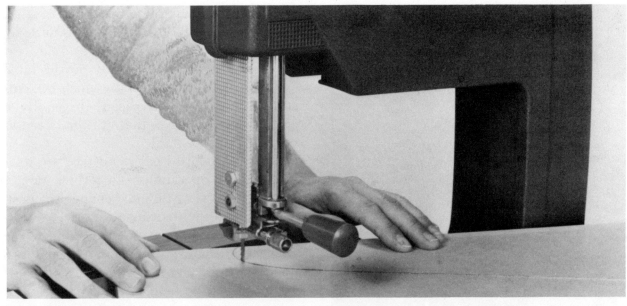

Illus. 23. In addition to making heavy sawing easy, the band saw is also adept at making lighter, more complex cuts. (Courtesy of Shopsmith, Inc.)

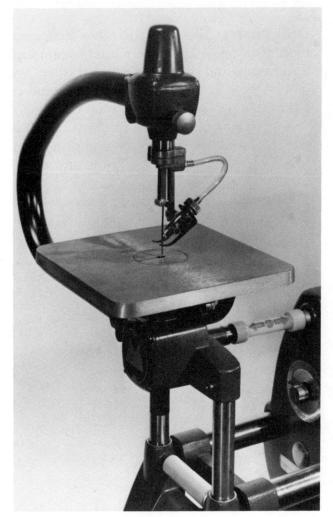

Illus. 24. A jigsaw is useful for complex trim sawing. (Courtesy of Shopsmith, Inc.)

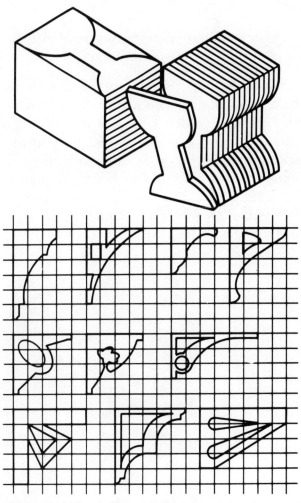

Illus. 25. (*Above*) The results of pad sawing and (*below*) patterns for use with band and jigsaws. Use the more complex patterns with jigsaws. (Courtesy of Shopsmith, Inc.)

Illus. 26. **Resawing is easy on a band saw. (Courtesy of Shopsmith, Inc.)**

Other stationary power saws are of little or no use to the birdhouse builder.

Jointers. A jointer's primary purpose is to make good joints possible. It planes a board's edge smooth (which is why it is sometimes called an edger) so that it will butt firmly against another board. It can also be used to plane the flat of a narrow board, though a full-scale planer does a better and faster job. The secondary job of a jointer is to cut rabbets (rebates), which are grooves cut from the edges of stock to enable other pieces of stock to fit into place. This kind of joint is more secure than a simple butt joint.

A jointer consists of a long narrow table divided in half by a slot into which the cutterhead fits. The cutterhead, driven by a motor, contains knives that cut the board as it is fed across the table.

Planing a board's edge and face are relatively simple operations. To form a rabbet (rebate), however, you must change the position of the guide (fence) so that only a portion of the knives are exposed. Then press the stock gently against the guide and feed it into the cutterhead. The passes for such cuts should always be held to a maximum of 1⁄8 inch to prevent chatter and possible feed problems. Also, you must always use a pusher of some sort to make certain your hands don't get near the knives.

Drill Presses. Like so many other stationary tools, drill presses aren't essential to building birdhouses and bird feeders, but they are more precise and faster than either a hand or a portable power drill. Bench-top models are very popular because power is plentiful while size is minimal, weight is low, and drill chuck size (1⁄2-inch) can accept almost any accessory.

Other tools, such as hand planers, stationary belt sanders (Illus. 27), and lathes, can be

Illus. 27. **Stationary belt sanders remove a lot of stock quickly and are handy when making more than one birdhouse from one or more patterns. (Courtesy of Shopsmith, Inc.)**

used to produce particular items with greater ease, to save money on finished wood products (the planer), or to make decorative spindles, but there is absolutely no requirement for them in making houses and feeders. Power tools can make building easier and more precise (Illus. 28), but every plan here can easily be made with hand tools, no matter what tools are shown in producing it.

Illus. 28. My Mark V is superb for birdhouse building, including the difficult removal of very thin strips of wood to square up stock.

5
JOINTS

Joints

Most of the constructions in this book require joints of one kind or another. Wood joints vary so widely that there are entire books written on the subject, and methods of fastening those joints vary almost as widely as the joints themselves. Be assured—there is little that you *must* know beyond the simple butt joint if you want to make good, solid birdhouses and bird feeders. Beyond that is experimentation and decoration. Several types of joints are shown in Illus. 29.

Butt Joint

A butt joint is nothing more than the point where the edge of one board meets and is fastened to another board, butting one another at a 90° or 180° angle. In a flat-butt joint, the boards meet edge to edge or edge to end. In a T-butt joint the boards meet edge to face.

The angle of the butt may change the name of the joint, as in a mitred joint in which the ends are *cut* at a 45° angle to the board's face (Illus. 30).

Butt joints may be glued, nailed, screwed, dowelled, or fastened with splines. Special brackets shaped as flat-surfaced Ls may also be used. Butt joints are the weakest, simplest, and most often used of all wood joints. While weak in comparison to joints designed to resist specific forces, a well-made butt joint is plenty strong when nailed, screwed, or glued.

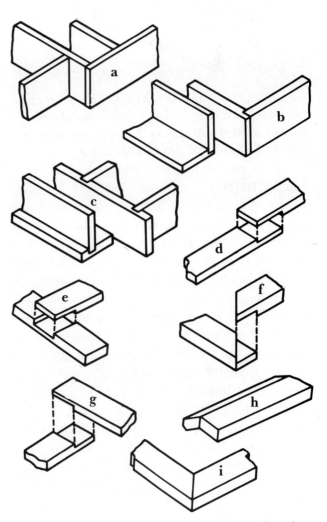

Illus. 29. Wood joints: (*a*) butt joints, (*b*) rabbets, (*c*) dado and groove, (*d*) end lap, (*e*) center lap, (*f*) mitred lap, (*g*) end lap, (*h*) bevelled mitre, (*i*) mitre. (Courtesy of Shopsmith, Inc.)

Edge fit is important: the straighter the edges of the two boards being joined, especially if glue is to be used, the stronger the joint will be.

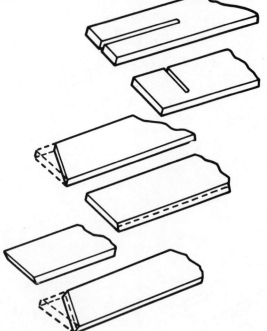

Illus. 30. Mitre and bevel cuts. The bevel cuts normally run lengthwise, though not always. Mitres always run across the grain in solid wood. (Courtesy of Shopsmith, Inc.)

Lap Joint

Lap joints come in several forms and are handy devices for fastening boards. They are somewhat stronger and not too much more difficult to make than butt joints. A lap joint is actually an overlap joint, in which portions of each are cut away so that the resulting joined surfaces are flush. (The joint need not always be smooth, as thin boards can be joined to thick boards, causing the lap notch in one board to be thinner, or nonexistent). Boards so joined can be glued, nailed, or screwed together for added strength. An end lap joint is composed of the meeting of the ends of two boards that have been cut away so that a level, smooth surface is formed, and the boards overlap. Lap joints, like butt joints, are useful in forming flat, wide boards; joining two boards at right angles with little chance of twisting; and forming boxes.

To form a rabbet joint, which is similar to a lap joint, cut away a portion of one edge of

a board so that another board can fit into it. Rabbets are used in a wide variety of ways. They are useful when attaching the back of a box or cabinet flush to the sides. They can also help form the top, sides, and bottom of boxes. The fitting of the back or other board into rabbets on all four side boards tends to help prevent twisting of the overall shape, so that corners remain square longer. Because board edges are hidden when inserted into the rabbet, this type of joint is common for concealing plywood and wafer-board edges in box making.

Dadoes

Dadoes are usually cut with a special blade on a table or radial saw. Dado blade sets have two special outer blades with chipper blades inserted between them, forming a device that cuts a groove (that runs with the grain) or a dado (that runs against the grain) into a board. Be sure to cut dadoes so the boards fit snugly and provide an exceptionally strong joint, especially when you're making bookshelves and drawer bottoms. To make dadoes for any birdhouse design add to the dimensions given at least the width of the dado for the sides being dadoed and add the depth of the dadoes to the bottom. It's preferable to add at least ¾ inch to the length to prevent the end from splitting off too easily. Lap and dado joints are often combined, as are rabbets and dadoes.

Mortise-and-Tenon Joints

These are among the most popular for the moderately advanced woodworker. When properly made in properly sized stock, just about no other joint can compare in strength. Some types that provide the greatest strength are rather difficult to make, and few woodworkers bother to carry out the intermediate steps by hand any longer, for those require a great deal of chiselling and chopping. Tenons are easy to cut since they are nothing more than rabbets or laps with three or more sides. Mortises, though, have to be drilled for depth and then chiselled to a finished, square shape. Today many people round the tenon ends and allow the mortise to retain its rounded corners, making a fit that is almost as good as the old square-shoulder mortise-and-tenon joint. This sort of joint would seldom be used in birdhouse construction, unless you decide to make a fancy post with an arm that could be joined using a mortise-and-tenon joint. You may, of course, employ this joint as a challenge or for decorative purposes.

Dowelled Joints

Dowelled, or pegged, joints are popular because they are both easy to make and quite strong. Choose one of two methods. Either form a butt joint first and then drill the holes from outside the joint through both pieces and finally insert the pegs or dowels. Or, perform the dowelling operation first. Mark the points to be drilled, drill the holes, insert the dowels, and then mark the opposing points, drill the holes to receive the dowels, and insert them. This operation can be simplified by using a tool known as a dowel point, or a template. Drill your first set of dowel holes, insert the dowel points of the correct size into that hole, and then press the unit into place against the piece to be joined. Tap firmly. The points on the little metal inserts will automatically mark the centers of the holes to be drilled into the new piece of material.

When making wood joints that require gluing, be sure to leave enough space for the glue. If you don't, it will either be forced out of the joint or the joint will split, weakening it badly. Leave enough space at the bottoms of the dowel holes, 1/16 inch or slightly less, so that excess glue is pushed there, not back out onto the work surfaces. After inserting the glue, give the dowelled boards no more than a fairly firm push into the holes. The neatness and strength of the job depends on leaving that small amount of space in the holes.

Splined Joints

Splined joints (Illus. 31) are usually made by inserting a small piece of stock or a metal fastener into the edges of a butt joint. By alternating the grain sides, you can not only

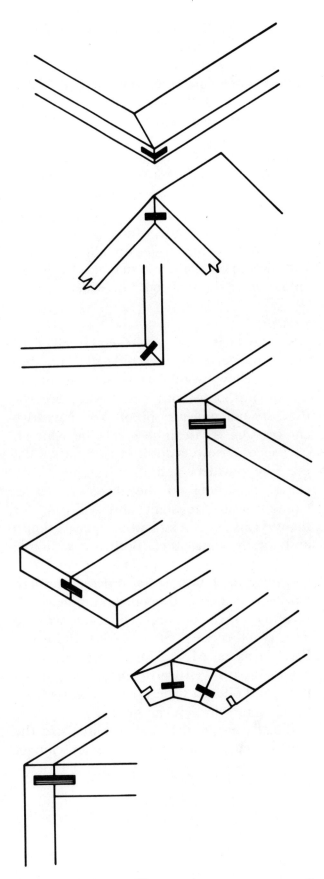

Illus. 31. Splines will strengthen many types of joints and are fairly easy to make and install. (Courtesy of Shopsmith, Inc.)

greatly widen boards this way, but solidly reduce warping and cupping, which is always a problem in wide stock. Splines are made of either ⅛-inch cutoff stock or plywood. If cutoff stock is used, the grain should run against the grain of the boards being joined. (If both grains run lengthwise, the spline, because it is so thin, will almost certainly split, breaking the joint.) Splined joints need to be glued, so be sure to leave room for the glue. To insert a spline, slice a groove with a standard circular- or table-saw blade, which usually gives a kerf about ⅛ inch wide. Should you use a carbide-tipped blade, you may need a thicker spline, since the kerf could be wider.

Glues

Glue may be inserted into several or all of the joints discussed. Neither hide glue nor aliphatic (yellow) wood glue, though, are of any use in birdhouses and bird feeders because they are not moisture proof. You have two choices. One is cascamite wood glue, which is packaged in powder form in two parts. First mix the powders and then combine with water, according to the directions. It is strongly water resistant and will last for many years. Resorcinol wood glue is liquid and totally waterproof. Both are available from a number of manufacturers and can generally be found in or ordered through hardware dealers and woodworking shops. (If no other source presents itself locally, write to The Woodworkers' Store, 21801 Industrial Blvd., Rogers, MN 55734, requesting their catalogue; it's well worth the money, all by itself, and offers a wide variety of glues from which your selection can be made.)

If nails are used to make joints, size the nails so that they are about three times longer than the thickness of the smaller of two pieces being joined. In most cases, you can even choose a shorter nail and produce a more than satisfactory joint. There's little need for the strength provided by using 2¼-inch nails to join a ¾-inch board to the edge of another, when you can possibly eliminate some problems by using 2-inch or even 1¾-inch nails. Nails, like screws, can be substituted for clamps when such joints are glued.

When nailing into end grains (or, for that matter, when placing screws into end grains), always try to either glue or add a nail or screw so the joint is stronger.

Joint making for houses and feeders, then, is not overly complex, though it may be made so if you desire. The plans provided here include simple, usually butt, joints. But changing most of them to more sophisticated (and more difficult to produce) wood joints would not be difficult. You can, if you wish, use finger joints or even dovetail joints.

The birds aren't likely to care one way or the other which joint is used, so it's up to you to decide. You may pride yourself on joint production, or it may worry you. A suggestion from a carpenter I once knew might prove helpful: if you don't like doing it, do it five times; if you love doing it, do it once. Of course, if your purpose is to create a few units, no matter how rough their appearance, and you never plan to do any other woodworking, then do it once.

Some birds even prefer rougher finishes. You may find that a nice, glossy painted finish on a birdhouse roof will keep that house unoccupied, while your roughly textured roofed place is always full. In the next chapter on finishing houses and feeders you'll find more details and options.

6
FINISHES

Finishes

For most of the woods suitable for bird constructions, no finish is necessary. They eventually weather to a nice grey color and last as long as or longer than most of us care to look at them. Finishes, then, become decorative instead of necessary.

Most finishes require renewal after a few years. If you paint a birdhouse, renewal may be delayed until the paint shows obvious signs of wear and tear. But with clear, matt finishes, you may not know just when refinishing is required. Most manufacturers recommend that their finishes be renewed at three-year or more intervals.

Steps to a Good Finish

Although finishing techniques for fine furniture are different from those for simple bird houses and feeders, some steps are common to both. These include setting nails below the surface and covering them with either glazier's putty or an exterior-use wood putty. For a smooth finish sand lightly, starting with a medium-grade paper and then changing to a fine-grade. Use a tack cloth to remove any traces of dust and coat with your choice of finish.

Paints

High-gloss paints tend to startle birds. So, at least for exterior surfaces, they're not recommended for bird houses or feeders. Use instead an exterior-grade flat paint to produce the colors and designs you might have in mind. All paints on today's market should be lead free, but just in case, check the paint container.

Good exterior-grade flat paints should last about five years. You might find the roof coat doesn't last as long if the birds house or feed there fairly often. But it is easy to clean and recoat.

Apply paints only to dry surfaces, out of the sun where possible, and use a brush of appropriate width (about 2 inches wide is sufficient for the structures described in this book). Follow the manufacturer's directions as to application and drying time, and you should have no problems.

Don't paint the surfaces on which the food is placed. The birds are likely to peck off the coating anyway, which means that the painting results in a waste of time, energy, and paint.

Stains

Select a good water- or oil-based stain and apply out of direct sunlight to a dry surface with a 2-inch brush. Make certain the stain contains no lead and follow the manufacturer's directions. Your results should be excellent.

Select, of course, only exterior-grade stains. Water-based stains for exterior woods do not present quite the same problems as interior water-based stains do, because you don't have to worry as much about raising the wood grain. Fine-furniture finishes applied over raised grains are not very attractive, and usually such stains require more work. The small amount of raised grain produced by using a latex (water-based) exterior stain is of no importance.

Most all exterior stains are designed to protect as well as color, so you don't need to apply a sealer after applying the stain.

Clear Finishes

The most useful clear finishes for bird houses and feeders are the polyurethanes, but for exterior use they are almost all high gloss and may send birds away from, rather than to, your houses and feeders. I would not recommend using any such exterior finish.

Preservatives

Wood preservatives may sound like a good idea for certain birdhouses and bird feeders, but actually, because these are such small projects, preservatives are probably more trouble than they're worth. It makes much more sense to select a naturally protected wood, like redwood or cedar. Their slightly higher price is more than offset by their longevity.

One feeder (Illus. 39) was built for me as a present some years ago by a friend. He built it entirely of cedar, including the shakes for the roof. It is just now about to be set up, after nearly eight years in outdoor storage. Other than a grey tone, there is no appreciable sign of weathering.

If you do decide to use a preservative, select one of the newer ones on the market. On February 1, 1985, the United States Environmental Protection Agency proposed a ban on the three major wood preservatives, which, as a result, brought several other substances to prominence on the market. All three banned substances—the pentachlorophenols, the arsenicals, and the creosotes—have been proven to be hazardous to the user's health. It is, though, nearly impossible to make wood preservative without its having some form of toxicity problem—skin irritation, genetic malformation, or cancer. Thus, when applying any of these materials, wear gloves and make sure the air is well-ventilated. Cut treated materials only while wearing goggles and a dust mask.

The best wood preservative I have found is made with mineral solvents. Other preservatives are made with water-based solvent. Some people now claim that water-based solvents are a bit better than the mineral-based ones, because wood is partly water, which enables the preservative to penetrate and bind better. In any case, use preservatives only when required and use them with care.

While you may not find evidence in the illustrations (46, 73, 76), those houses and feeders I've built from wafer board are covered with a stain to simulate the color of weathered wood and provide protection from the elements. Some companies rate their wafer board for exterior use, but staining improves its durability even more and improves its appearance, too.

7
BIRDHOUSE
DESIGNS

Birdhouse Designs

In some ways, the actual building of a birdhouse is easier than getting the right kinds of birds to arrive and take up residence. Poor positioning of a perch, too large (or small) an entry hole, too large a structure, and a dozen other things can cause problems with the types of birds that arrive at your houses. Feeders that are the wrong shape and type have similar problems attracting the intended species. Of course, if a particular bird doesn't inhabit your area of the country, then all the houses and feeders you build can't attract one. But otherwise, proper design helps keep birds you don't want to support away, while protecting those you do want. (See Illus. 32–69.)

Predators

Consideration needs to be given to protection as well as comfort when designing bird structures. You'll have to think of such things as the neighborhood cat population, and how and if you'll be able to protect nesting birds from them. Choosing appropriate materials and placing the structure correctly are both important. For pole-mounted feeders, materials are even more important than otherwise, for cats can readily climb the slenderest wood pole, but they have great trouble with even the thickest plastic support. Thus, a 1½-inch to 2-inch-diameter PVC pipe is often the best pole support. If you decide to use a wooden pole, you need to form a metal cone and slip it over (or fasten it around) the pole to guard against climbing predators (Illus. 32).

I don't mean to single out cats as the only predators. Squirrels and rats can be worse. My house and yard are usually full of cats and instinct is instinct. Even a lazy house cat will occasionally grab a bird that's unwary, nesting, or feeding. It somehow detracts from my enjoyment of watching birds in the yard when I realize that at any moment they could become a snack for one of my fully fed felines. Barn cats and wandering cats tend to be quite adept at grabbing birds and locating feeders where groups of birds are less wary than usual.

Squirrels and rats both can cause more problems than cats. Squirrels cause most problems at feeder sites, while rats may be a big problem at nesting sites, where they destroy eggs. In fact, rats sometimes kill the parent bird as well, when night falls and the bird is sitting on the eggs.

Rat control seems to be a problem in rural as well as urban areas, and the main protections are cleanliness, sealing off of food sources, cats, and hope. I have been fortunate in controlling such problems rapidly. When my family moved into an abandoned farmhouse some 50 miles south of Madison, Wisconsin, there was a large and partially full dairy barn less than 100 yards away. It was full of hay and feed, not cows. We had four

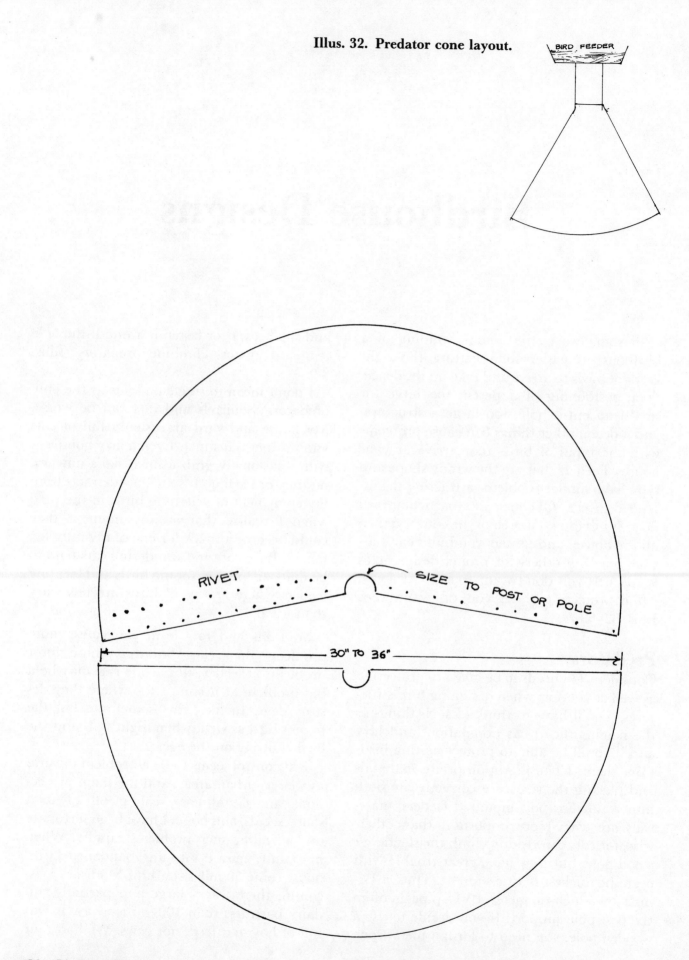

cats at that time, and within two weeks no more rats and very few mice appeared. There was also a fine population of barn owls, which also helped to control the rodents.

Siting

The attraction to a birdhouse of a particular species of bird depends in large part on the house's location. Among the four nesting categories of birds, one type is likely to come into your yard and take up residence.

Water birds, such as herons, ducks, gulls, some grackles, and blackbirds, aren't totally aquatic, but they do seem to strongly prefer marsh or swamp areas. They're nearly impossible to attract.

Ground nesters, those species that like to nest in the ground or in cliffs, are also nearly impossible to attract to a yard house. Among these are the wild turkey, pheasants, grouse, juncos, some sparrows, some doves, and the hermit thrush. All you can do to attract them is to leave strips of grass or brush along fences and in uncut and unburned areas so they'll have safe nesting sites.

In the third group are more possibilities, including some songbirds, though they tend to prefer nesting in trees and shrubbery. These can often be lured into your yard if you plant the type of shrubbery they prefer. This group includes catbirds, finches of several kinds, orioles, robins, cardinals, mockingbirds, hummingbirds, thrashers, and a few others. If a portion of your yard has vines, low trees, and bushes, then you can expect to see these species. Cardinals, especially, prefer such cover. They have settled in the low shrubbery that has grown over a fence in my yard over the years, cavorting with flickers and other ground feeders.

Also among this group are shelf nesters, who do not care for the totally enclosed cavity of a birdhouse. They are enticed by a weather-protected structure that doesn't hinder access. Robins, phoebes, and barn swallows are among those who nest on shelves. They often build nests in sites that don't seem sensible (including the upper parts of several chimney flues in my old house).

Cavity nesting birds are the ones most birdhouses are designed to attract. This group includes familiar birds, such as chickadees and several woodpeckers, starlings, martins, wrens, tree swallows, titmice, nuthatches, bluebirds, flickers, and some lesser-known species, such as the wood ducks, sparrow hawks, some owls, and a number of others. As you can readily see, birdhouse sizes and possible sites for nesting must vary according to the species you want to attract.

Birdhouse Styles

The housing styles preferred by various species are fairly well known, and some bird associations even make recommendations accordingly. But don't be too surprised to find a house occupied by a different species with somewhat similar tastes. The American Bluebird Society, for instance, recommends certain sizes if you want to attract bluebirds and discourage other species. You may wonder why fairly specific dimensions are given in these construction plans for housing birds, when in the wild birds have to take what they can get. The difference is you are trying to change the bird's behavior—to get it to nest in an unnatural site—at least in part for your own pleasure. At the same time, you are attempting to provide an optimum breeding ground for birds you would like to see multiply.

Bluebirds provide a good example because there is increasing competition from house sparrows, among other birds, in the wild (or semiwild) environment they normally inhabit. Although the recommended entry hole for the bluebird house serves very well for the sparrow, the sparrow has larger broods so will not usually steal the nesting area from the bluebird (Illus. 34–41).

As the size serves to keep sparrows away from the bluebird house, so its location will work to keep wrens out. Because wrens prefer shrubbery, place the box somewhat closer to a cleared area and try to make sure a tree or a good-size shrub is within 100 feet. The brushy patch will give the fledgling birds a place to land when they first try their wings, especially if you turn the house so the entrance hole is in a direct line with the tree or shrubbery.

Wrens aren't as much of a problem to attract as bluebirds. They will nest almost anywhere, from an old shoe to a tin can, requiring less planning and work, which makes housing easier to supply. You may have some trouble keeping them out when you'd rather have other birds, though sometimes people have found difficulty in attracting them.

Generally, if you provide a house high enough to accept a 1½-inch-diameter entry hole some 6 inches from a floor that measures about 4 × 6 inches, then you'll get wrens. They'll nest quite close, too, not needing housing more than 100 feet or so apart. It's best, however, to place the entry holes for their birdhouses so that prevailing winds don't blow in during cold weather.

Correct sizing of the birdhouse dictates whether or not the birds you start attracting remain to nest. Obviously, if they investigate and can't get in, then they will move on. But it's difficult to tell why they also move on when the entry hole appears sufficiently large, the box of more than good size for the parent bird, and the location nearly ideal.

Birdhouse Sizes

Standard sizes have been observed over the years and are accepted by most people who build and categorize housing for birds. The United States Department of the Interior has published a chart of appropriate sizes for birdhouses. The chart, however, does not include all possible house sizes, which can vary widely. Entry holes, however, cannot vary. If you make the entry hole too large, your desired birds will probably be displaced by larger birds. Smaller holes usually keep larger birds out, but you can't always bet on smaller birds being less aggressive than the species you are trying to attract. In such cases, take what you can get and supply another residence.

The distance above ground (or water) of the birdhouse or nesting shelf is also impor-tant. If the house is not in an appropriate spot, you will fail to attract the species you want. For example, the house wren prefers a house that is no more than 10 feet from the ground, while the hairy woodpecker prefers a house no less than a dozen feet from the ground. Oddly enough, by providing dual nesting sites some 20 or 30 feet above the ground, you have a good chance of attracting owls and hawks. Both are hunters of the same type of feed, especially small rodents. But because the owls hunt at night and the hawks by day, there is no real competition (unless the area is short on rodents). Hawks, though, tend to prefer more open ground than owls, and so trees bordering a field are probably going to be preferred by hawks, and the inner trees in a wooded area by the owls (Appendix C, page 124).

Nesting Materials

After building and placing a nesting box, shelf, or house, you can do more than simply feed the birds that now gather around. Since nesting materials aren't always easily obtainable for a particular species, try placing the necessary items near the structure to encourage them to stay.

Various birds want and need different items for nesting materials, so you can soon be assured of seeing the various kinds of birds picking over your pile of twigs, hopping about the small mud puddles you have created or the bits of wool, fluff, and feathers you have placed in strategic locations.

Barn swallows, robins, phoebes, and some thrushes greatly appreciate the mud for their nests. In mud-free weeks and months, an old garbage-pail lid or shallow pan full of moist dirt will help them. Place it where the birds can get to it easily, but not where it's readily accessible to the entire household, particularly pets and children. Wrens will fly off with bits of dried twig, while swallows seem to prefer bits of light-colored fluff, like stuffing from old pillows and mattresses, which is excellent in small pieces. Vireos, robins, song sparrows, finches, cedar waxwings, and orioles will make good use of lengths of twine, grass, wood shavings (you should have a decent supply after building a few feeders and houses), and strips of fabric.

To present such materials to your birds, drape them over shrubs, or if your garden is more formal, nail a small basket or other container to a tree and add to the offerings daily or when possible. The pieces should be no longer than about 8 inches. Birds can carry longer pieces, but some materials are strong enough to form nooses that could cause problems to the birds you want to help. Replenish the supply through the end of the summer in most areas. This will take care of late nesters and those species that have more than a single brood each season.

It's best not to let materials build up and moulder in the birdhouse. It isn't good for birds to start nesting in mouldy materials. You'll find that those who have more than a single brood per season have healthier broods if you clean the nest out of the box after each group has left. Also check the nests for lice and mites. If they are found, dust the nest box with 1 percent rotenone powder.

Winter Shelter

While nesting boxes are in use, usually during breeding seasons, it's not uncommon for some songbirds to winter over, in which case they need some other form of shelter to survive in cold and windy weather. In some cases, the parent birds or other birds will simply use the nesting boxes for such shelter, but roosting boxes can be a help in areas (north of South Carolina, for example) where winters are long and harsh. Make the roosting box about 10 inches square and from 30 to 36 inches tall. Provide an entry hole some 3 inches in diameter facing south or away from prevailing winds and place ¼- or ⅜-inch dowels inside for perches, staggering them from side to side well down in the box. Protect it from predators, as you would a nesting box, and place it about 10 feet from the ground. (Here you're not modifying behavior so much as providing assistance in dire need.) These rather large boxes can hold many birds in cold weather, and they may well make survival possible where it might otherwise be unlikely.

Winter assistance for songbirds doesn't stop with simply providing breeding-time assistance and cold weather shelter for increasing numbers of birds. As more and more farms are sold for housing developments, birds are losing a primary source of feed. So during the winter it's a good idea to provide birds with a substitute. The following chapter covers feeder construction and filling. Much that applies to the building and location of birdhouses also applies to the construction of bird feeders, but some species have special requirements.

Birdhouse designs begin on the next page.

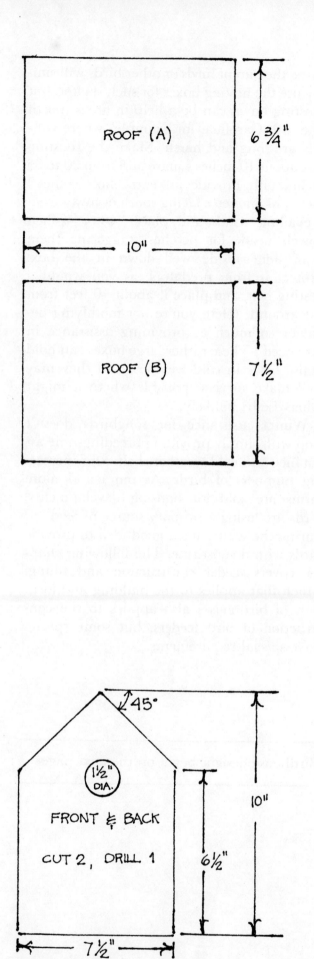

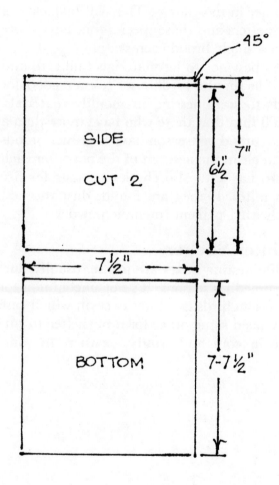

ROOF (A)

6 3/4"

10"

ROOF (B)

7 1/2"

45°

SIDE

CUT 2

7"

6 1/2"

7 1/2"

BOTTOM

7-7 1/2"

45°

1 1/2" DIA.

FRONT & BACK

CUT 2, DRILL 1

10"

6 1/2"

7 1/2"

Illus. 33. Plain birdhouse. This no-frills birdhouse is quite easy to make. Make all cuts, including angles, as shown, and then nail the bottom to the front and one side. Next, attach the back and the other side. And finally, attach the roof using 1¼-inch × No. 6 brass wood screws, to facilitate cleaning.

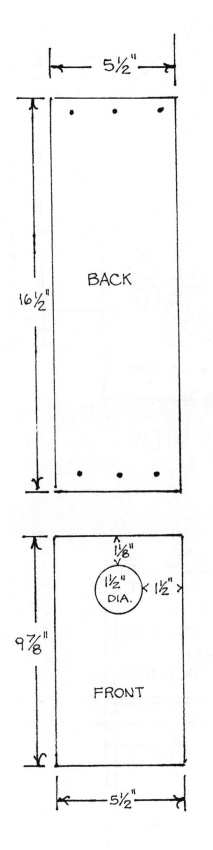

5½"

16½"

BACK

9⅞"

FRONT

5½"

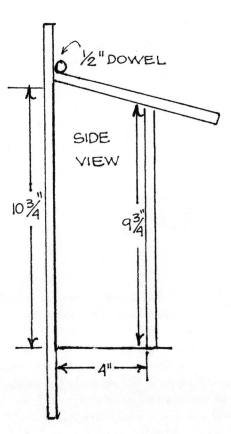

½" DOWEL

SIDE VIEW

10¾"

9¾"

4"

Illus. 34. One-board bluebird house. Place the dowel at the junction of roof and back to help keep water out and to help hold the roof on. Attach a cleat, a 3½" × ¾" × ¾" piece of wood, also to help hold the roof and to serve as a force friction fit at the front.

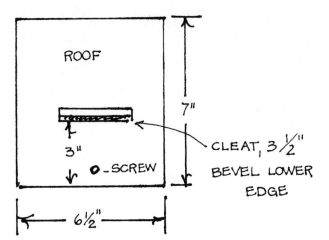

ROOF

7"

3"

O-SCREW

CLEAT, 3½" BEVEL LOWER EDGE

6½"

1½" DIA.

1⅛"

1½"

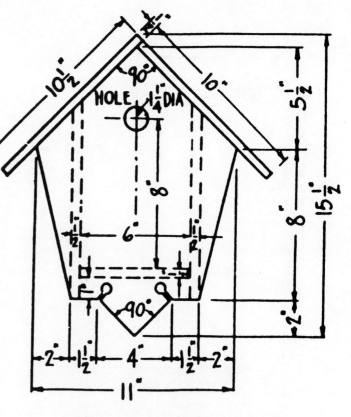

FRONT VIEW

Illus. 35. Bluebird house. Sides are 6 inches wide by 10 inches high. The bottom is 6 inches square. The top left roof piece is 10½″ × 9″, and the opposite roof side is 10″ × 9″. The back, at its widest point, measures 11 inches, and overall length is 15½ inches. The dashed lines in the drawing below represent the top edges of the sides, which are cut at a 45° angle. (Courtesy of Stanley Tools)

NOTE
SCREW ROOF IN PLACE TO
PERMIT CLEANING. USE
1¼″ #6 F.H. BRASS SCREWS

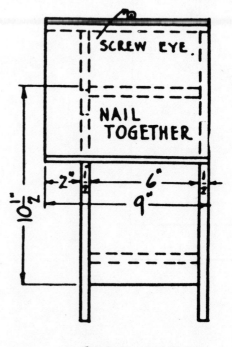

SIDE VIEW

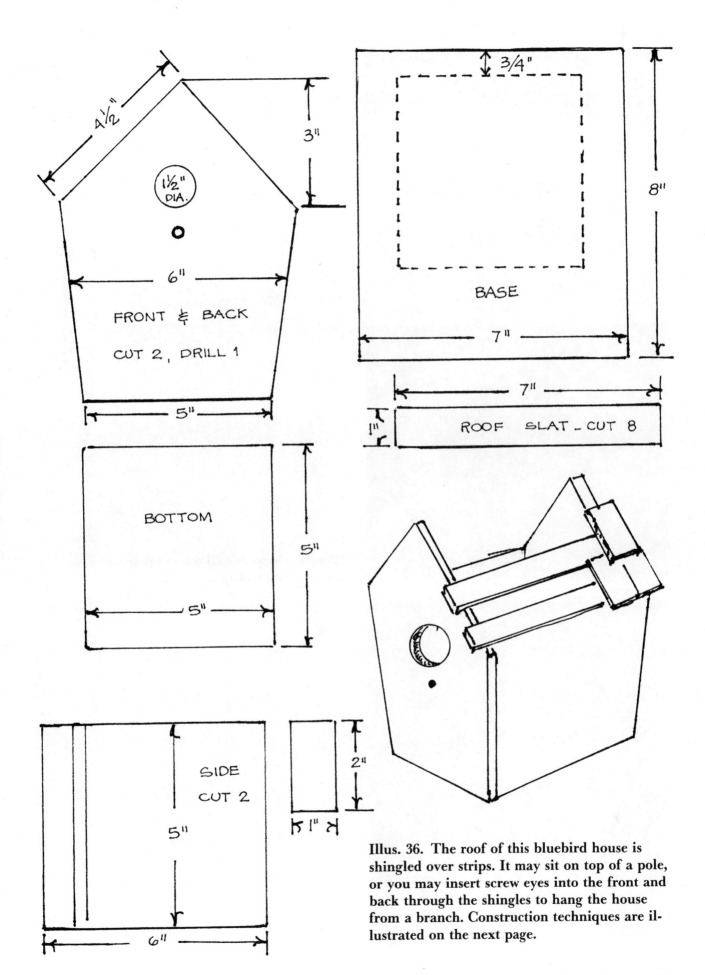

3/4"

BASE

8"

7"

7"

1"

ROOF SLAT – CUT 8

4½"

3"

1½"
DIA.

6"

FRONT ⅋ BACK

CUT 2, DRILL 1

5"

BOTTOM

5"

5"

5"

SIDE

CUT 2

5"

6"

2"

1"

Illus. 36. The roof of this bluebird house is shingled over strips. It may sit on top of a pole, or you may insert screw eyes into the front and back through the shingles to hang the house from a branch. Construction techniques are illustrated on the next page.

Illus. 37. First fit the shingles.

Illus. 38. Now, install a 6 mil poly sheet to prevent roof leakage.

Illus. 39. The completed house has a front that's removable for cleaning.

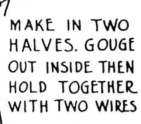
MAKE IN TWO
HALVES. GOUGE
OUT INSIDE THEN
HOLD TOGETHER
WITH TWO WIRES

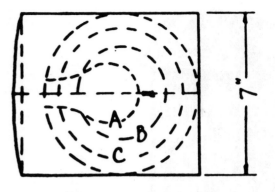
TOP VIEW

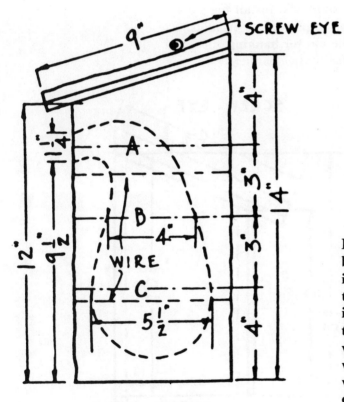
SIDE VIEW

Illus. 40. Rustic birdhouse for swallows and bluebirds. Using a seasoned log of pine 14 inches long and 7 inches in diameter, cut it so that the back is 14 inches and the front is 12 inches. Cut the log in two pieces and gouge out the interior to the dimensions shown. Then wire the two pieces together with galvanized wire. Cut a 9″ × 7″ piece of redwood or slab wood and nail it on as a top, attaching a screw eye to hang the nest. (Courtesy of Stanley Tools)

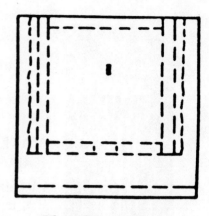

TOP VIEW

Illus. 41. Another rustic house for swallows and bluebirds. Using slab wood, cut the back 12½ inches high by 5 inches wide. Cut two sides 10½ inches high by 6 inches wide, and then cut an angle at the top so the front edges are 8 inches high. Cut the front 5″ × 8″ and drill a 1¼-inch entry hole 6⅝ inches up from the bottom. The back can be cut at 45° angles, as shown. The bottom is 5 inches square. Assemble the sides, front and back, install the bottom, and nail the top in place. Use 4d nails. Place a screw eye on the top for hanging. Screw top in place to facilitate cleaning.

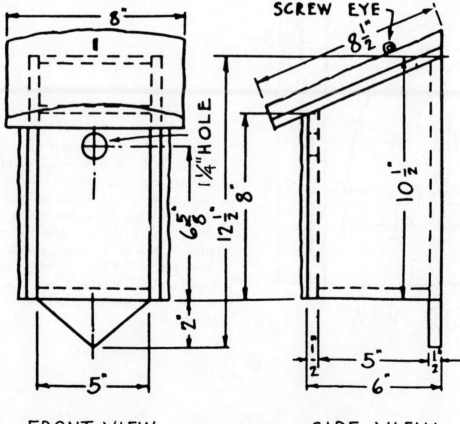

FRONT VIEW   SIDE VIEW

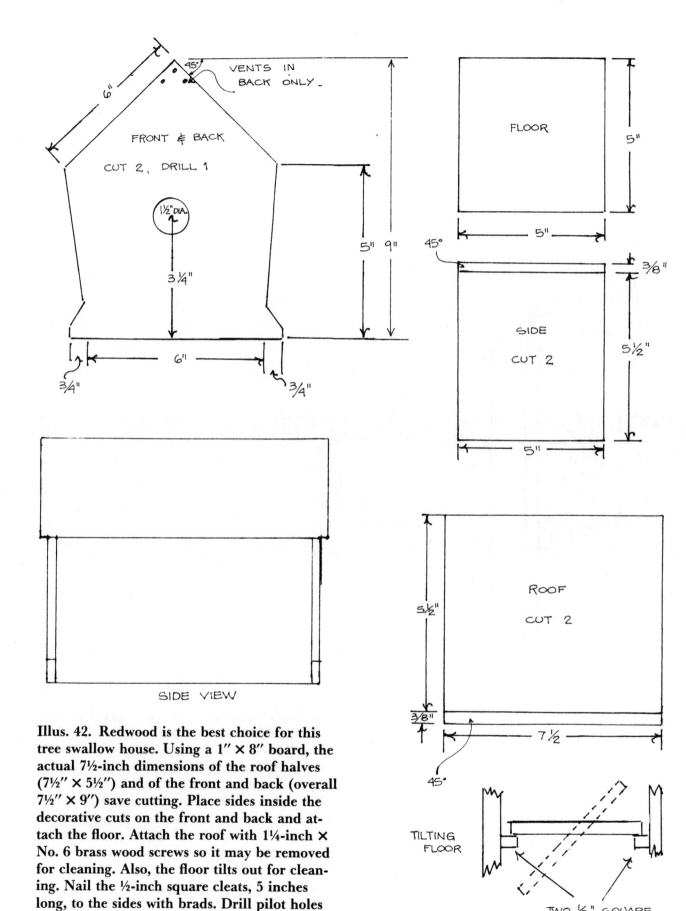

6"

45°

VENTS IN
BACK ONLY.

FRONT & BACK

CUT 2, DRILL 1

1½" DIA.

3 ¼"

5"   9"

6"

¾"   ¾"

FLOOR

5"

5"

45°

3/8"

SIDE

CUT 2

5½"

5"

SIDE VIEW

ROOF

CUT 2

5½"

3/8"

7½"

45°

TILTING
FLOOR

TWO ½" SQUARE
CLEATS

Illus. 42. Redwood is the best choice for this tree swallow house. Using a 1″ × 8″ board, the actual 7½-inch dimensions of the roof halves (7½″ × 5½″) and of the front and back (overall 7½″ × 9″) save cutting. Place sides inside the decorative cuts on the front and back and attach the floor. Attach the roof with 1¼-inch × No. 6 brass wood screws so it may be removed for cleaning. Also, the floor tilts out for cleaning. Nail the ½-inch square cleats, 5 inches long, to the sides with brads. Drill pilot holes in this very light material, or it will split as you nail.

WASTE

← 3½" →

SCOOP,
CARVE, OR
GOUGE OUT

CONSULT CHART
FOR ENTRY HEIGHT

← 8" →

16"

24"

FLOOR PLUG
(a) CLEAT
(b) OUTER CAP
(c) INNER BOTTOM

a   b   c

FLOOR PLUG

Illus. 43. This woodpecker log works best with a log that measures 7 inches in diameter and about 18 inches long. Cut the back off the log, making the width 3½ inches and gouge out the interior, leaving at least a 1-inch or thicker wall. Drill the entry hole and attach the roof after the backboard is in place. Use 4d finishing nails or 1¼ inch × No. 6 brass wood screws. The floor is removable. Assemble it from the three pieces a, b, and c. Nail the square inner bottom to the round cap. Then nail on a cleat for easy twist off and cleaning. A cleat nailed to the backboard helps hold it in place.

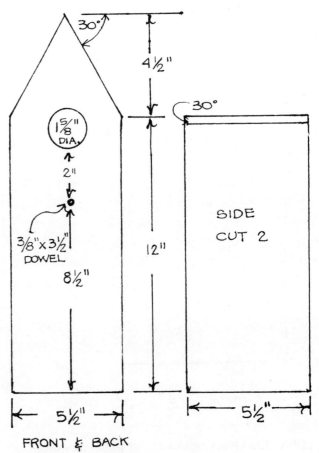

4½"

30°

1 5/8" DIA.

2"

⅜" × 3½" DOWEL

8½"

5½"

FRONT & BACK
CUT 2, DRILL 1

30°

12"

SIDE
CUT 2

5½"

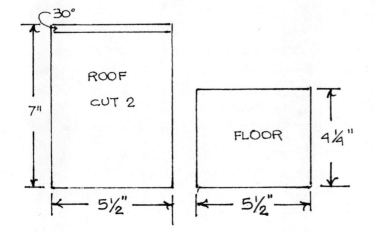

30°

ROOF
CUT 2

7"

5½"

FLOOR

4¼"

5½"

Illus. 44. Hairy woodpecker box. Use 1″ × 6″ redwood (actual size is ¾″ × 5½″) and 1½-inch × No. 6 brass wood screws. Assemble sides, front, and back before cutting out the floor, which should measure 4¼ inches.

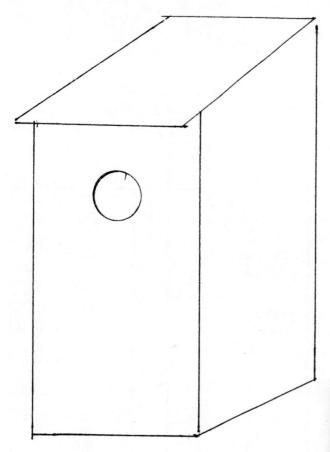

FRONT & SIDE VIEW

Illus. 45. One version of the pileated wood-pecker house. (See diagram in Illus. 47.) This style house can be mounted on a pole. Be sure that the top section of the pole is jointed so that it can be lowered. Make the joint about 6 to 8 feet above ground, using two redwood splice boards that have been attached through the post with 6″ × ¼″ bolts, two above and two below the joint. By removing the lower car-riage bolts, you can tilt the pole down towards you.

Illus. 46. Another version of the pileated woodpecker house. This style house can be at-tached to a tree or post.

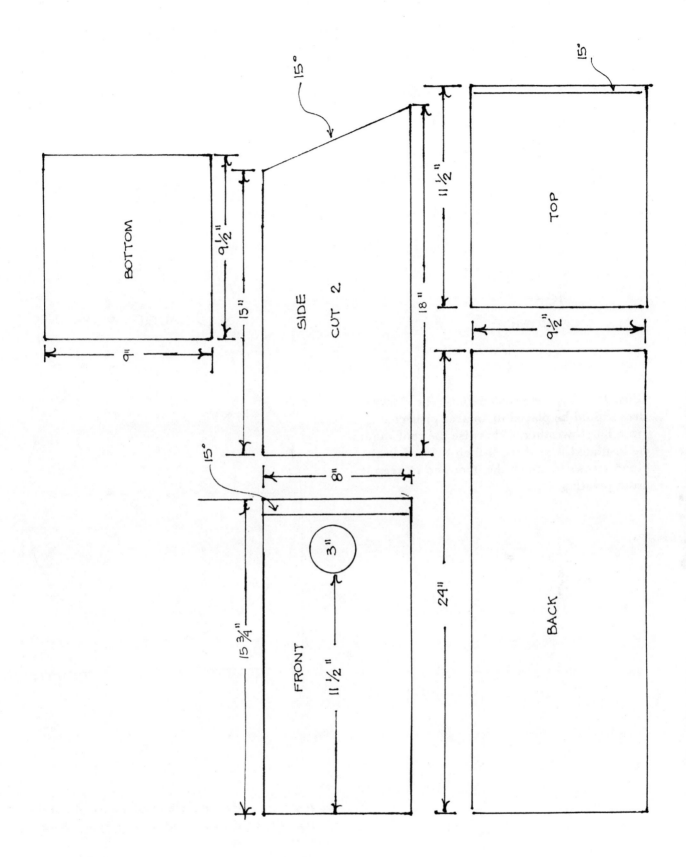

Illus. 47. Diagram for pileated woodpecker house. Note: dimensions given correspond to the house shown in Illus. 46.

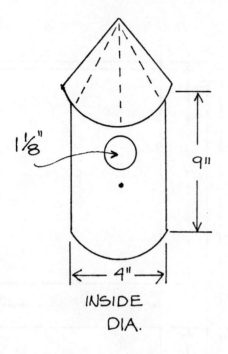

INSIDE
DIA.

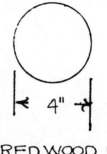

RED WOOD PLUG

FOR FLOOR

Illus. 48. This cone-roofed house for chicka-dees should be placed in an area protected from harsh weather. Otherwise the roof should be insulated. Use three ¾-inch × No. 6 brass wood screws to attach the floor and to keep it from pivoting.

24-GAUGE ALUMINUM

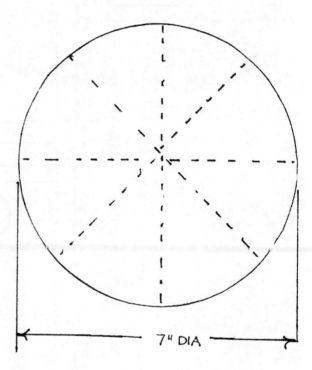

(*Opposite*) **Illus. 49.** Chickadees are about the friendliest birds around, so supplying them with a nesting house is a good idea. This model is designed for easy construction. Choose redwood or cedar. Attach two cleats to the bottom, and then insert a single screw into the front and another into the back, running through and into the cleats. Bottom removal for cleaning thus is a two-screw removal job.

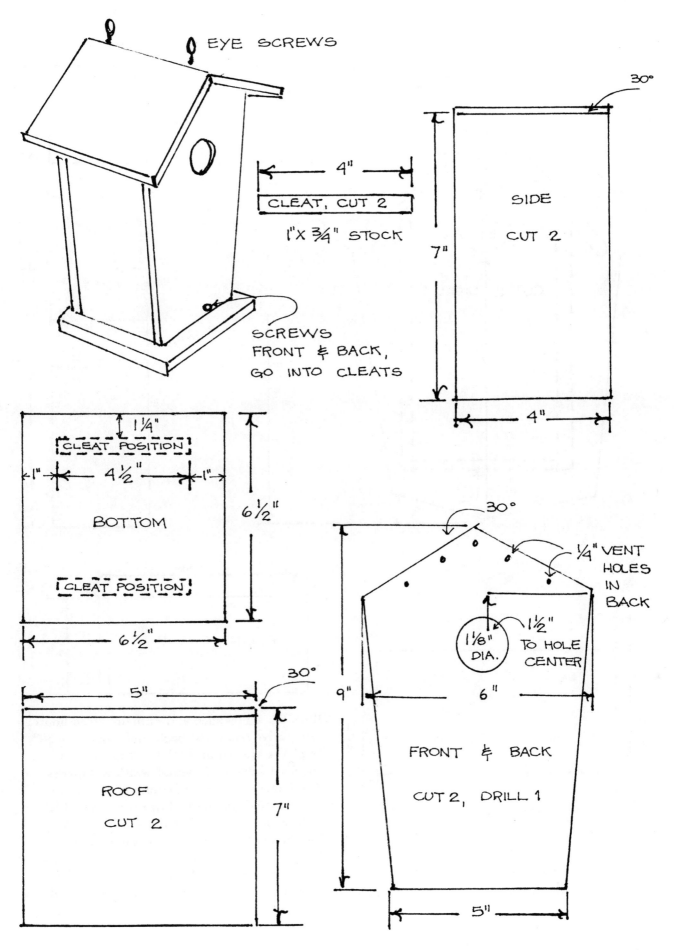

EYE SCREWS

CLEAT, CUT 2

1" X 3/4" STOCK

4"

30°

SIDE

CUT 2

7"

4"

SCREWS
FRONT & BACK,
GO INTO CLEATS

1 1/4"

CLEAT POSITION

1"   4 1/2"   1"

BOTTOM

6 1/2"

CLEAT POSITION

6 1/2"

30°

1/4" VENT
HOLES
IN
BACK

1 1/8"
DIA.

1 1/2"
TO HOLE
CENTER

9"

6"

FRONT & BACK

CUT 2, DRILL 1

5"

30°

ROOF

CUT 2

7"

5"

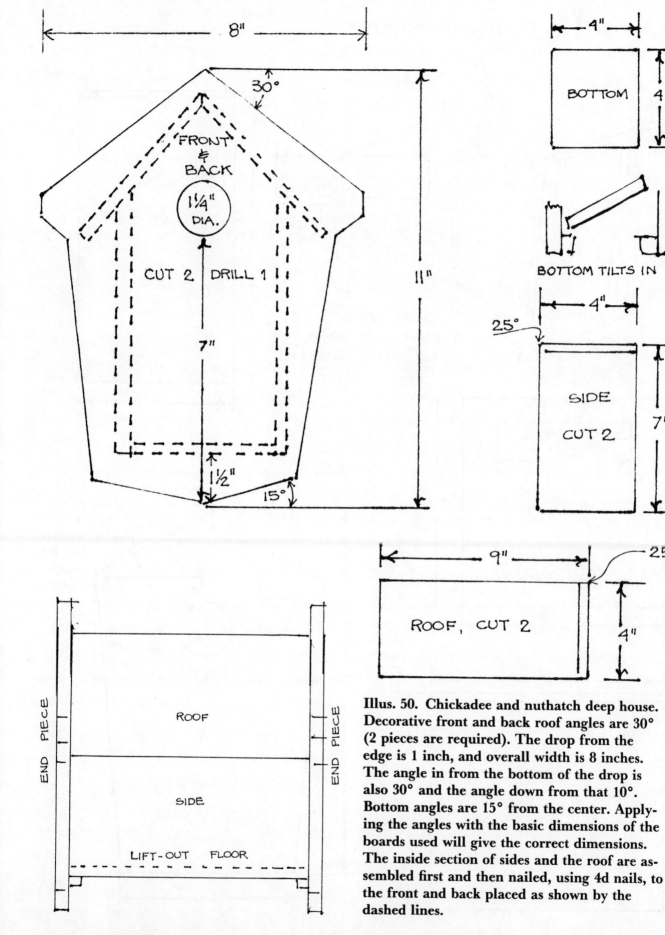

8"

30°

FRONT & BACK

1¼" DIA.

CUT 2 DRILL 1

7"

11"

1½"

15°

4"

BOTTOM

4"

BOTTOM TILTS IN

25°

4"

SIDE

CUT 2

7"

9"

25°

ROOF, CUT 2

4"

END PIECE

ROOF

SIDE

LIFT-OUT FLOOR

END PIECE

Illus. 50. Chickadee and nuthatch deep house. Decorative front and back roof angles are 30° (2 pieces are required). The drop from the edge is 1 inch, and overall width is 8 inches. The angle in from the bottom of the drop is also 30° and the angle down from that 10°. Bottom angles are 15° from the center. Applying the angles with the basic dimensions of the boards used will give the correct dimensions. The inside section of sides and the roof are assembled first and then nailed, using 4d nails, to the front and back placed as shown by the dashed lines.

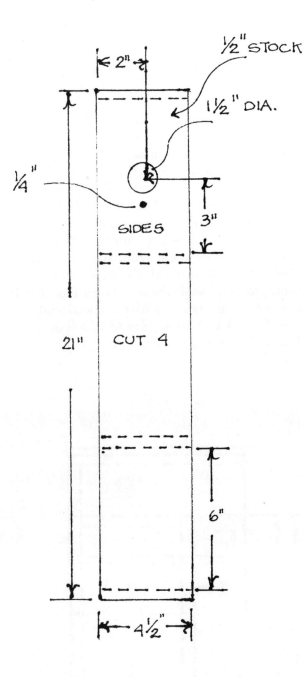

½" STOCK

1½" DIA.

2"

¼"

SIDES

3"

21"

CUT 4

6"

4½"

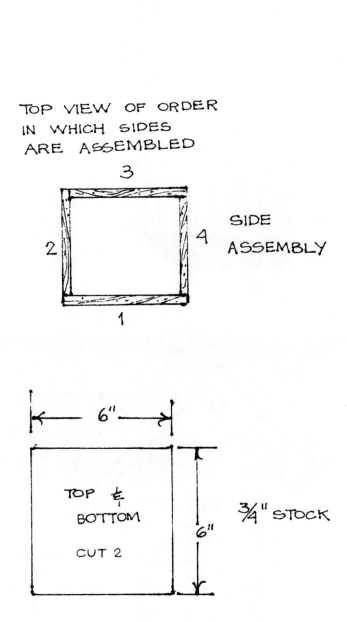

TOP VIEW OF ORDER
IN WHICH SIDES
ARE ASSEMBLED

3

2   4

1

SIDE
ASSEMBLY

6"

TOP &
BOTTOM

CUT 2

6"

¾" STOCK

Illus. 51. Wren, chickadee, and nuthatch tower. Drill holes so that there is one per side and one per level (total of 3) to allow birds some privacy. Otherwise all sections will not be filled.

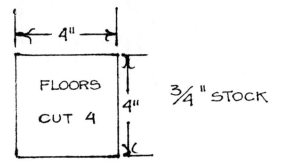

4"

FLOORS

CUT 4

4"

¾" STOCK

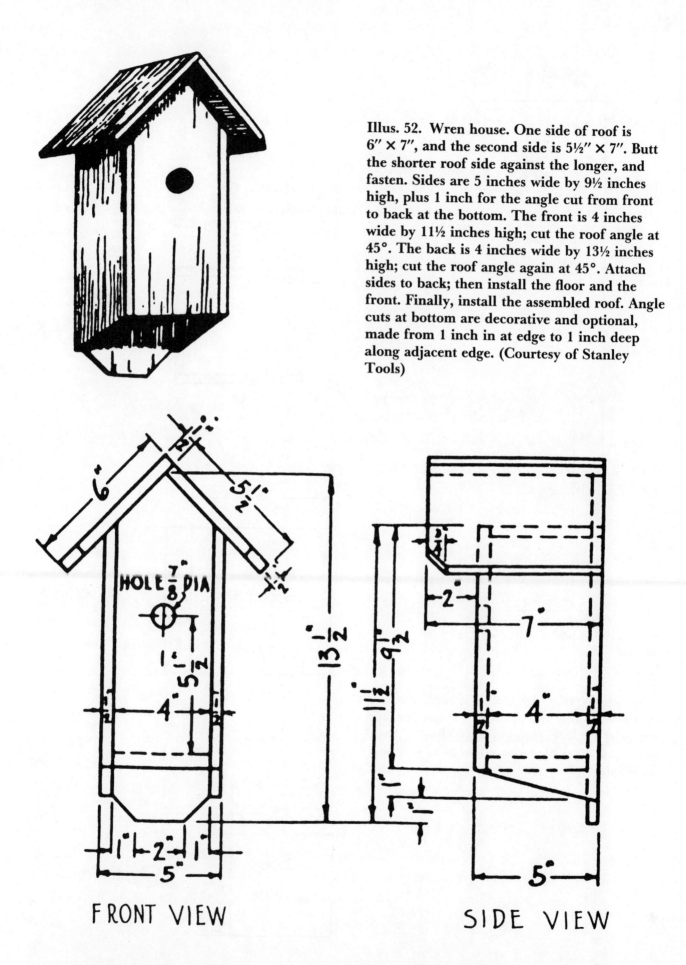

Illus. 52. Wren house. One side of roof is 6″ × 7″, and the second side is 5½″ × 7″. Butt the shorter roof side against the longer, and fasten. Sides are 5 inches wide by 9½ inches high, plus 1 inch for the angle cut from front to back at the bottom. The front is 4 inches wide by 11½ inches high; cut the roof angle at 45°. The back is 4 inches wide by 13½ inches high; cut the roof angle again at 45°. Attach sides to back; then install the floor and the front. Finally, install the assembled roof. Angle cuts at bottom are decorative and optional, made from 1 inch in at edge to 1 inch deep along adjacent edge. (Courtesy of Stanley Tools)

FRONT VIEW

SIDE VIEW

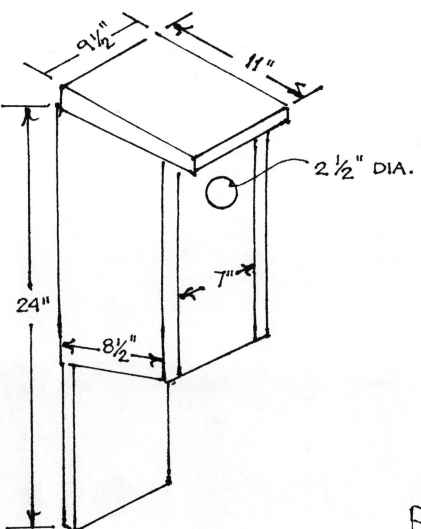

2 ½" DIA.

Illus. 53. Swing-front flicker house. The back is 24 inches high by 7 inches wide; the roof is 11 inches long by 9½ inches wide; and the sides are 8½ inches wide by 18 inches tall. Cut at a 15° angle at the top. The front is 7 inches wide with a 2½-inch-diameter entry hole placed 12 inches from the bottom edge. Actual height is measured after the sides are assembled to the back, and the top edge is cut on a 15° angle. (The top edge should be about 17 to 17½ inches for rough-cut purposes.)

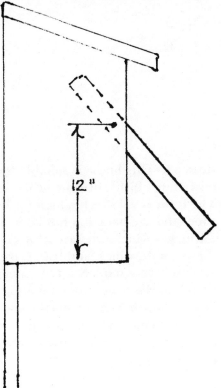

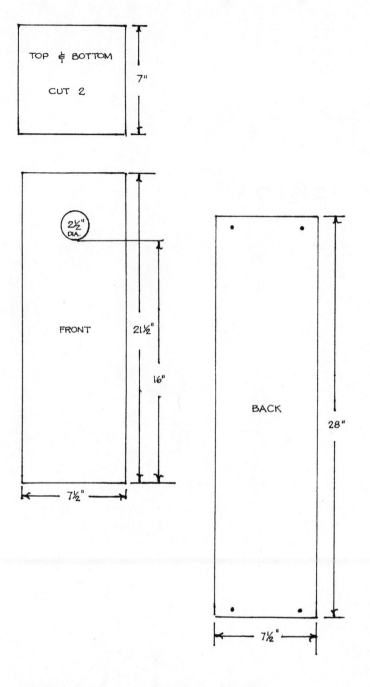

TOP & BOTTOM

CUT 2

7"

2½" DIA.

FRONT

21½"

16"

7½"

BACK

28"

7½"

Illus. 54. This house is suitable for flickers, fairly large birds, because of its ample size. The front is 21½ inches high by 7½ inches wide, and the back is a full 28 inches high by 7½ inches wide. Sides are 7″ × 21½″ (not shown in drawing), and both top and bottom are 7 inches square. Start by assembling the sides and the front around the top and bottom, using 1¼-inch × No. 6 brass wood screws. Drill the entry hole and place the unit on the back, 3 inches up from the bottom. Into both the top and bottom of the back drill two ⅛-inch holes, one at each corner, 1 inch in and ¾ inch up, for mounting onto a tree or post.

Illus. 55. Redwood flicker house assembled.

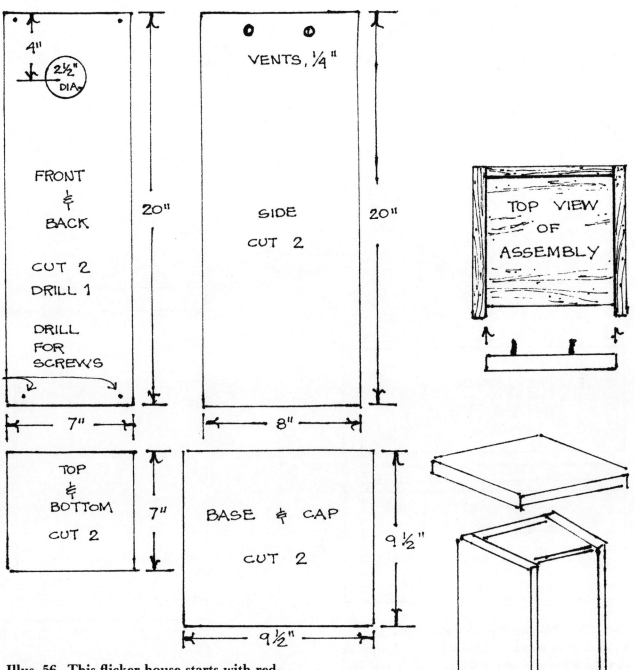

4"

2½" DIA.

FRONT
&
BACK

CUT 2
DRILL 1

DRILL
FOR
SCREWS

20"

7"

VENTS, ¼"

SIDE
CUT 2

20"

8"

TOP VIEW
OF
ASSEMBLY

TOP
&
BOTTOM
CUT 2

7"

BASE & CAP
CUT 2

9½"

9½"

Illus. 56. This flicker house starts with redwood boards, 1″ × 10″. Cut out base and cap. Cut out sides and drill the vents near the top of each. Cut out the front and back and drill a 2½-inch-diameter entry hole into the front. For top and bottom, cut two pieces 7 inches square. Assemble the top, bottom, both sides, and the back. Then add the base and cap. Use 1¼-inch × No. 6 brass wood screws. Then attach the front by inserting two screws into the top and two into the bottom. This makes the front easily removable at the end of each nesting season so you can clean out the box. Add 2 to 3 inches of wood shavings to give the flickers a good start on their nest.

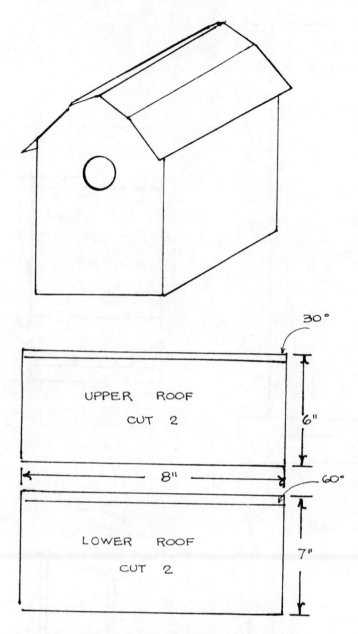

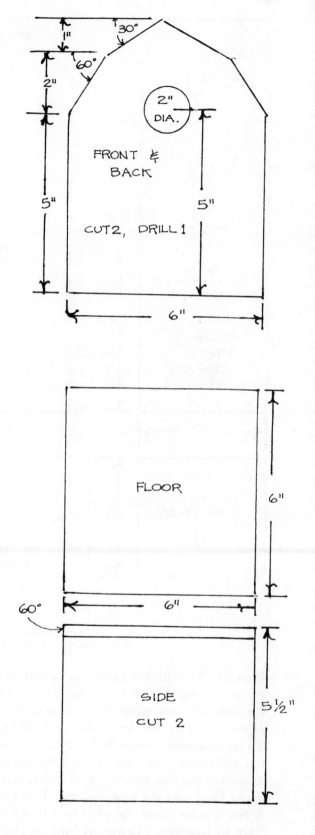

Illus. 57. This gambrel-roofed birdhouse can be altered to suit a number of birds simply by changing the size of the floor, roof pieces, and entry hole. The design is fairly simple. Use redwood and 1¼-inch × No. 6 brass wood screws.

The front and back pieces are identical, except that the 2-inch-diameter entry hole is drilled into the front. Make the angle cuts (60° and 30°) and then cut out the four roof sections. Cut a 30° angle at each upper edge of each upper roof and cut a 60° angle at each upper edge of each lower roof. Assemble the roof bottom parts first, with the 60° angle cuts facing upwards. Then place the upper roof parts, with the 30° angle cuts, at the ridge of the house.

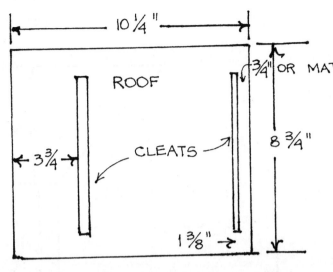

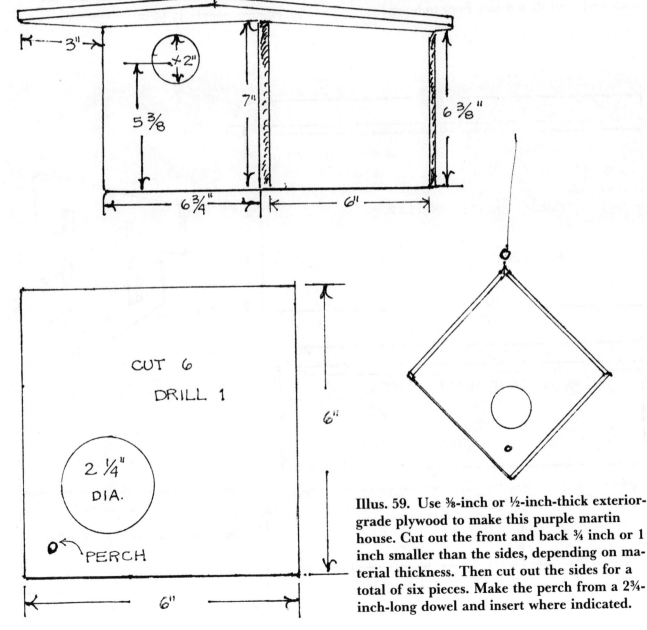

ROOF

CLEATS

10¼"

¾" OR MATERIAL THICKNESS

3¾"

8¾"

1⅜"

3"

2"

5⅜"

7"

6¾"

6"

6⅜"

CUT 6

DRILL 1

2¼"
DIA.

PERCH

6"

6"

Illus. 58. This house-finch box is made of ¾-inch-thick wood, preferably redwood. Front and back are, respectively, 6¾ inches wide by 7 inches high and 6¾ inches wide by 6⅜ inches high. Sides are 6″ × 7″ at the front, 6″ × 6⅜″ at the back. The bottom is 6″ × 6¼″. The roof is 10¼″ × 8¾″, with two 6″ × ¾″ × ¾″ cleats attached to the inside. These provide a friction fit for the roof and make the roof easy to lift out when cleaning is necessary.

Illus. 59. Use ⅜-inch or ½-inch-thick exterior-grade plywood to make this purple martin house. Cut out the front and back ¾ inch or 1 inch smaller than the sides, depending on material thickness. Then cut out the sides for a total of six pieces. Make the perch from a 2¾-inch-long dowel and insert where indicated.

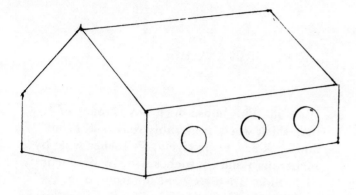

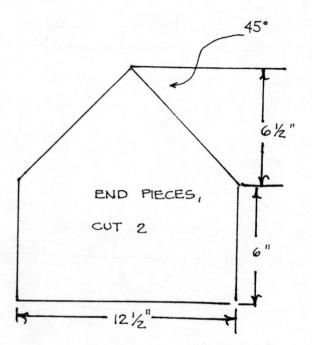

45°

END PIECES,

CUT 2

6½ "

6 "

12½ "

Illus. 60. Six-martin house. Cut out roof, sides, front, and back and assemble. Cut out floor 20″ × 13½″ and partitions. Make the partition slots 2¼ inches deep. Attach partitions to floor with nails and then attach floor to house.

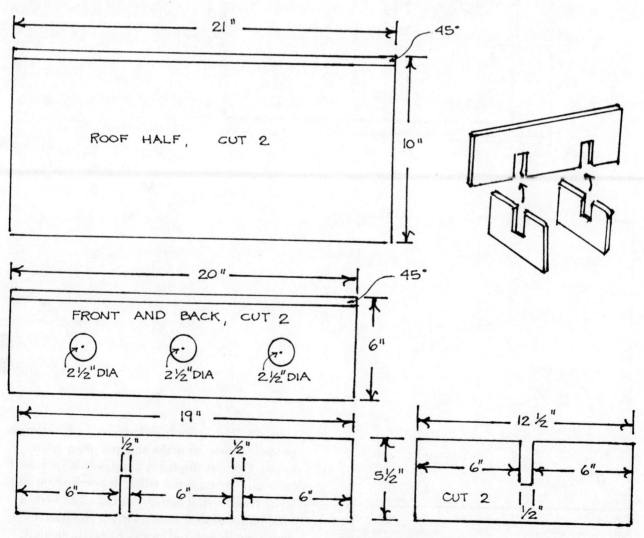

21 "

45°

ROOF HALF, CUT 2

10 "

20 "

45°

FRONT AND BACK, CUT 2

2½"DIA   2½"DIA   2½"DIA

6"

19 "

½ "   ½ "

6 "   6 "   6 "

12½ "

6 "   6 "

5½ "

CUT 2

½ "

PARTITIONS

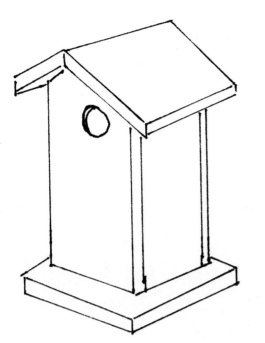

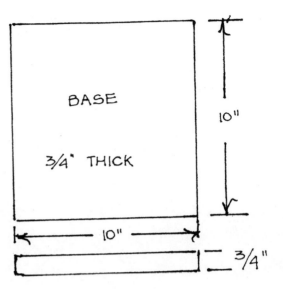

BASE

3/4" THICK

10"

10"

3/4"

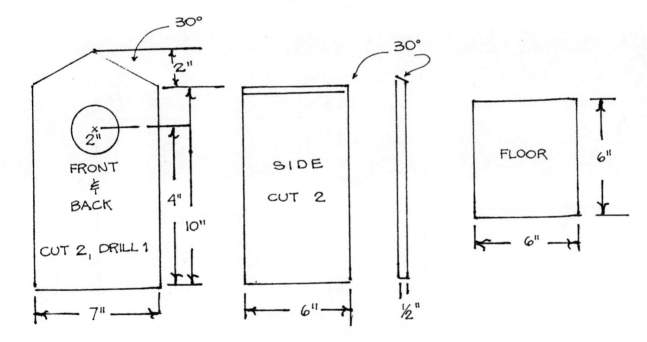

30°

2"

2"×

FRONT
&
BACK

CUT 2, DRILL 1

4"

10"

7"

SIDE

CUT 2

6"

30°

1/2"

FLOOR

6"

6"

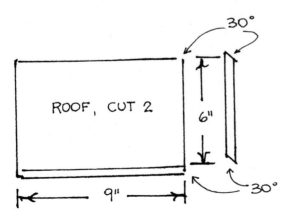

ROOF, CUT 2

30°

6"

30°

9"

Illus. 61. Flycatcher house. Start assembly by
screwing the floor into the center of the base.
Next, assemble the front and one side, and
then do the back and the other side, using
nails or screws. Finally, add the roof pieces,
screwing them into place with 1¼-inch × No. 6
brass screws so that the roof can be removed
for cleaning.

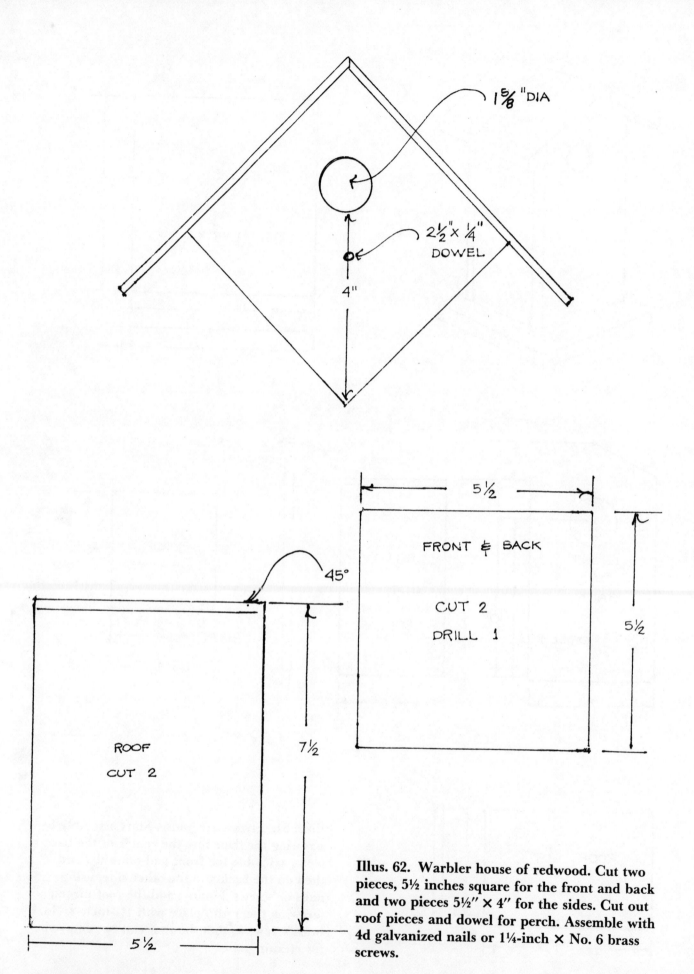

1 $\frac{5}{8}$ " DIA

2 $\frac{1}{2}$" × $\frac{1}{4}$" DOWEL

4"

45°

5 $\frac{1}{2}$

FRONT & BACK

CUT 2

DRILL 1

5 $\frac{1}{2}$

7 $\frac{1}{2}$

ROOF

CUT 2

5 $\frac{1}{2}$

Illus. 62. Warbler house of redwood. Cut two pieces, 5½ inches square for the front and back and two pieces 5½″ × 4″ for the sides. Cut out roof pieces and dowel for perch. Assemble with 4d galvanized nails or 1¼-inch × No. 6 brass screws.

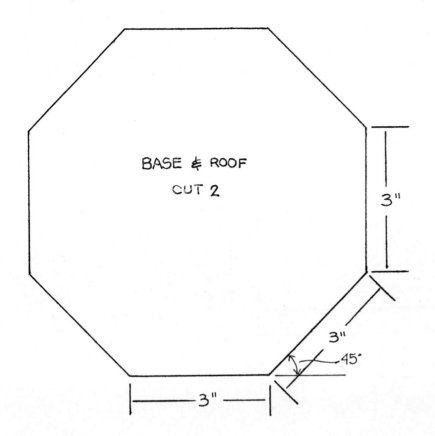

BASE & ROOF
CUT 2

3"

3"

45°

3"

Illus. 63. Octagonal swallow house. A table
saw may be necessary to make the 22½° rip
cuts. Eight sides are required; drill one for
entry. Use ¾-inch-thick stock.

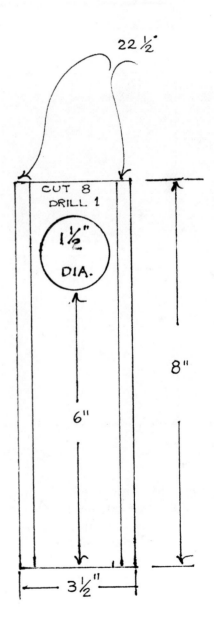

22 ½°

CUT 8
DRILL 1

1½"
DIA.

8"

6"

3½"

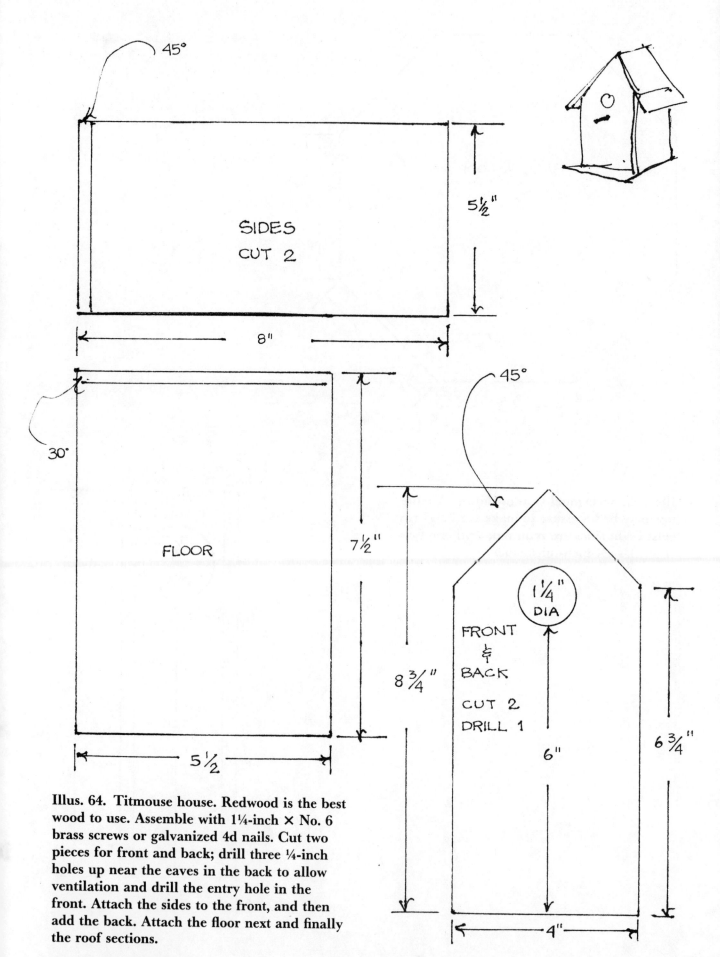

45°

SIDES
CUT 2

5½"

8"

30°

FLOOR

7½"

45°

1¼"
DIA

FRONT
&
BACK

CUT 2
DRILL 1

8¾"

6"

6¾"

5½

4"

Illus. 64. Titmouse house. Redwood is the best wood to use. Assemble with 1¼-inch × No. 6 brass screws or galvanized 4d nails. Cut two pieces for front and back; drill three ¼-inch holes up near the eaves in the back to allow ventilation and drill the entry hole in the front. Attach the sides to the front, and then add the back. Attach the floor next and finally the roof sections.

Illus. 65. Nesting box for robins, song sparrows, barn swallows, catbirds, thrashers, and phoebes. Cut ½-inch-thick redwood 9″ × 10″ for the top. The back is 8″ × 10″, and the one attached side is 6½ inches wide and 10 inches high at the rear and 8 inches high at the front. The floor is 6″ × 7½″, and two strips, 1″ × 6″, are nailed to the floor on the two open sides. (Courtesy of Stanley Tools)

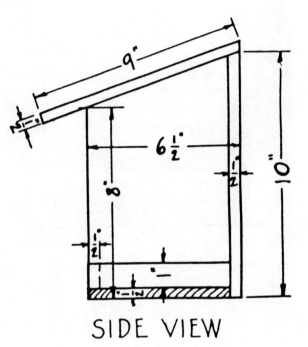

SIDE VIEW

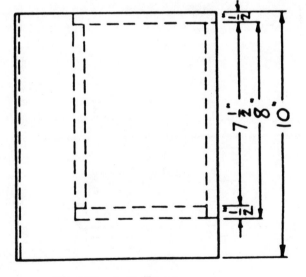

TOP VIEW

Illus. 66. Robin nesting box, assembled.

SIDE
CUT 2

15°

6½"

7½"

4"

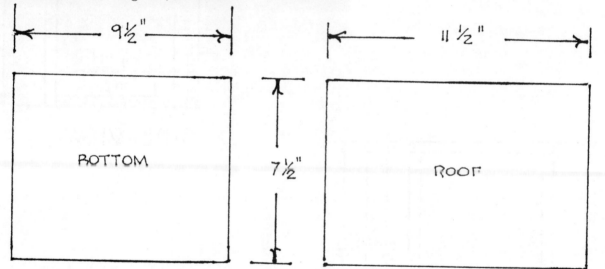

9½"

BOTTOM

11½"

ROOF

7½"

Illus. 67. Robin nesting box. Cut out the bottom from a 1″ × 8″ redwood board (actual width is 7½ inches). Cut out the roof and back from the same board. Cut out the sides from the board's 7½-inch width. Attach the sides to the bottom, flush to the back and outside edges, and then attach the back. Finally, screw on the roof using 1¼-inch × No. 6 brass wood screws.

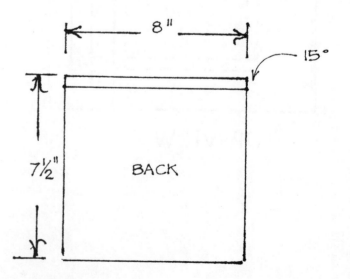

8″

15°

7½"

BACK

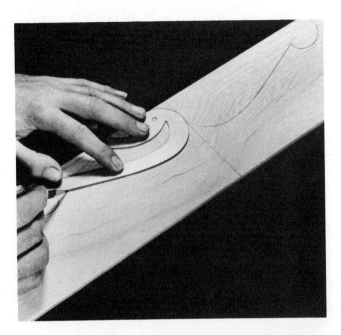

Illus. 68. A French curve facilitates the drawing of decorations. (Courtesy, Shopsmith, Inc.)

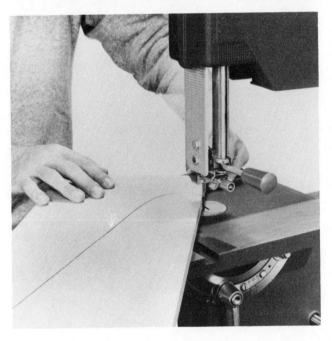

Illus. 69. A band saw can cut simple designs proficiently. (Courtesy, Shopsmith, Inc.)

8
BIRD-FEEDER
DESIGNS

Bird-Feeder Designs

Bird feeders (Illus. 71–90) may be as simple or as complex as you wish to make them. There's nothing wrong with using just a simple window ledge for feeding. In fact, after finding my two cats asleep in front of the stove, I just now put out some bread crumbs on the porch sills. In this case, the sills aren't really wide enough to serve a large number of birds, but the porch is long enough and consists mostly of windows, so that this method is somewhat successful. But by using such a procedure I have to wash down the aluminum clapboards at least twice a year. Birds are not neat feeders.

Another problem with any window area is that no matter how frequently a flock of birds seems to come to such a feeder, some birds fly into the glass by accident. Most of the time, the bird is only dazed a little; but other times it may be seriously hurt, in which case the bird is in danger if a predator is nearby.

Leaving outside screens in place can help avoid such an accident, though today many types of windows offer only inside screening. Lightweight curtains are also helpful. A third problem is the easy access for other creatures like squirrels, chipmunks, and even mice. Still, after all considerations, you should probably offer the feed in another area of the yard.

The bird table is the simplest type of construction. It is made of nothing more than a flat board nailed or otherwise attached to a pole or post that is then placed in the ground.

Or you can make the table portable and a bit more complex by adding legs so it won't tip over.

To make this simplest of feeders, start by cutting some form of moulding or small straight board for a rim to keep feed from falling off the board. Then insert three nails (10d galvanized) into the board and the top of the post. If you're using a PVC plastic post, use a floor fitting to attach the board with screws to the feeder. Then cement the fitting to the post. In either case, the feeder should be at least 6 feet above the ground, which means a post of at least 8 feet in length in most areas. The board can also be attached to a windowsill area, but the many problems this presents are only slightly offset by the addition of more space for feed.

Drill a few holes in the board for drainage, since there is no roof to keep the rain off. Now you have an attractive feeder that will last through many winters.

Any feeder serves best if it has the same protection from predators as you would give a birdhouse. Thus the metal cone, a plastic pole, or long wires for hanging are all good ideas (Illus. 32 and 70).

Squirrels are a nuisance and seemingly unavoidable. I don't know of any totally effective deterrent except care in hanging the feeders. Predator guards (Illus. 70) will help some, but these acrobatic little animals can get into places cats only dream of, can eat a huge amount of grain, and will then move on

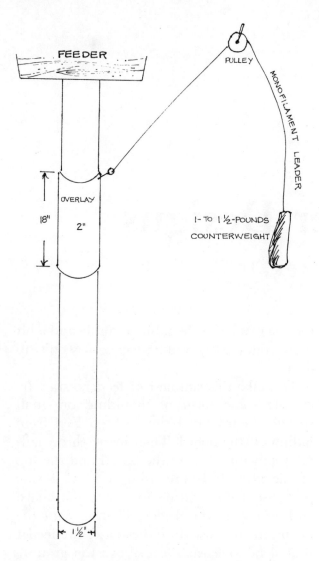

FEEDER

PULLEY

MONOFILAMENT LEADER

OVERLAY

18"

2"

1- TO 1½-POUNDS
COUNTERWEIGHT

1½"

Illus. 70. This predator slide works when a predator reaches the 18-inch-long overlay pipe section of PVC (polyvinyl chloride). Before the feeder is attached to its pole, slip on the overlay pipe. The inside diameter should be at least ¼ inch larger than the pole. Attach a screw eye to the top, near the edge, and run a wire or monofilament leader through a pulley attached to a tree or another pole at the same height as the top of the pole. Attach the wire to a counterweight that is 1 or 2 ounces heavier than the overlay pipe. When a cat, squirrel, or raccoon puts its weight on the overlay, the counterweight rises, and the overlay pipe slides down to the ground. Once the predator's weight is removed, the overlay is pulled up to its original position by the counterweight. The wire should be just long enough to enable the overlay to slide to the ground. Attach the pulley for the counterweight to any available stable structure or tree nearby. Make sure it is at least as high as the raised side.

until you refill the feeder. Even if you locate and obstruct the old route, they rapidly find a new one. A few, very few, squirrels can rapidly denude any feeder no matter how fast you fill it. Figure on at least some loss of feed to squirrels, triple that amount, and you should come close to the amount of feed you need, even with protection.

Most grain feeders for birds are nothing more than roofed-over board feeders that are open on one, two, or three sides (or in some cases all four sides).

Certain types of bird food, though, are not appropriate for board feeding. If you feed grains and occasionally some stale cakes or bread, the board feeder more than suffices, but in severe weather a bird's diet requires more.

Birds require suet in cold weather, and often they don't get it either through home feeding or in the wild. You need not serve suet, as such, though it's about the easiest way to supply the birds with fat. You can mix birdseed and bacon grease, mould the mixture into balls, and hang them from tree limbs to provide birds a complete diet in winter.

Another method is to mix the seed in warmed grease. Loop one end of a piece of twine and then drop it into the mixture. Pour the mixture with the looped twine into the bottom half of an old milk container. Set it in the refrigerator until it congeals, and then hang it with the unlooped end of twine from a branch. The weather, of course, must be cold enough during the day to maintain the congealed mould.

Another solution for cold-weather feeding is a hollowed out half log that is filled with a mixture of seed and grease and hung from a tree. If you attach ends to the log half, you can use the feeder in milder weather.

Some time ago, I found the best suet feeder of all for true suet (Illus. 88). It's nothing more than a length of cord tied to some hardware cloth (aluminum or galvanized wire cloth with a large—usually ¼-inch or larger—mesh) that is wrapped around the suet. The hardware cloth accomplishes three things: it secures the twine to keep the suet hanging in place; it gives the birds a place to perch; it forces the birds to ration themselves to relatively small pecks at any one time. Birds usually deplete the hanging grease patties and logs far too quickly for you to be sure that all of the birds in your garden are getting an equal share.

Placing feeders is similar to placing birdhouses in some ways and totally unlike it in others. Protection from severe weather (if for no other reason than to keep the seed from blowing free) and protection from predators are both necessary. You don't, however, need to give as much attention to size and location as you do with houses and nesting boxes. After all, in this case you're doing the bird a favor, not the bird you, so modifying its behavior is less essential. Still, some things need to be kept in mind.

Birds are less likely to feed when close to humans. At first you should place the feed at some distance from the house. Place feeders away from where snow is likely to accumulate. A 4-foot pile of snow under a 6-foot pole makes it hard for you to approach the feeder and far easier for predators and pests to arrive. Keep the feeder low enough so you don't need a ladder to fill it. Placing a nesting shelf for a hawk or owl some 30 feet up is fine, but it is inconvenient to climb that distance each day to fill a bird feeder.

Otherwise, feeders may be hung from tree limbs, hung from limbs supported by posts, placed on posts directly, or otherwise set around as you might wish. In fact, you can feed directly on the ground from time to time. Some birds prefer to feed from the ground, as you'll see from those around the base of any feeder catching the spills (juncoes, among others, seem to be inveterate ground feeders). If you can't keep the feed above the snow or if the ground is too muddy, place a piece of plastic or old tarp on the ground for a good feeding surface that's easy to remove and easy to clean with a hose.

There are also specialty feeders. The one for the hummingbird heads the list. If you live where hummingbirds don't feed, don't waste time and energy trying to attract them. If you are lucky enough to live in a feeding area, you'll find that this delightful little anomaly requires only a sugared water diet, which naturally enough needs a special feeder. Still, nothing fancy is needed. Use a very small, slender plastic vial and tip it at about a 30° angle. Place it where you like, using wire through the edges, and add a cone-shaped bit of plastic in a bright color to the open end. The cone-shaped plastic seems to imitate a flower, which is what nectar-feeding birds, such as hummingbirds, are attracted to, so they'll sip away through the cone, while their wings blur madly.

Feeding hummingbirds isn't a cold weather activity, as far as I know, so be sure to change the sugar-water mixture every couple of days to prevent fermentation. Mix two parts water to one part sugar to make the nectar.

If no birds appear, try either planting more and brighter flowers or placing the feeder closer to the flower beds. Generally, hummingbirds are found only in the Southeast and Southwest, with reportedly the widest number of species in the Southwest.

After building and setting the feeding stations, you can review the kinds of feed that might go into them during a typical winter feeding period (pages 115–18). Many kinds are available, and the price for any one type varies greatly from area to area.

Bird-feeder designs begin on the next page.

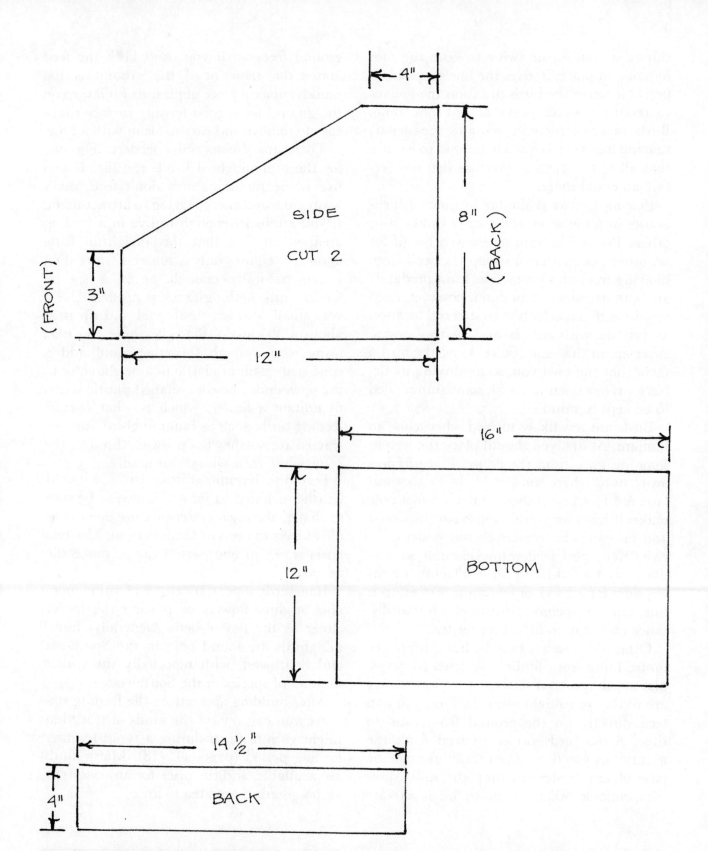

Illus. 71. Window feeder. Cut out pieces from ½-inch-thick exterior-grade plywood. Assemble with 2d galvanized nails. Attach sides to bottom, and then attach the low back to the inside of the sides, resting on the bottom. Coat plywood edges with a sealer. Nail or screw the feeder directly onto an exterior windowsill with nails so it can be removed easily when worn. Use brass wood screws, 1-inch × No. 6, and place them 4 inches apart along the back edge, just about an inch inside the back.

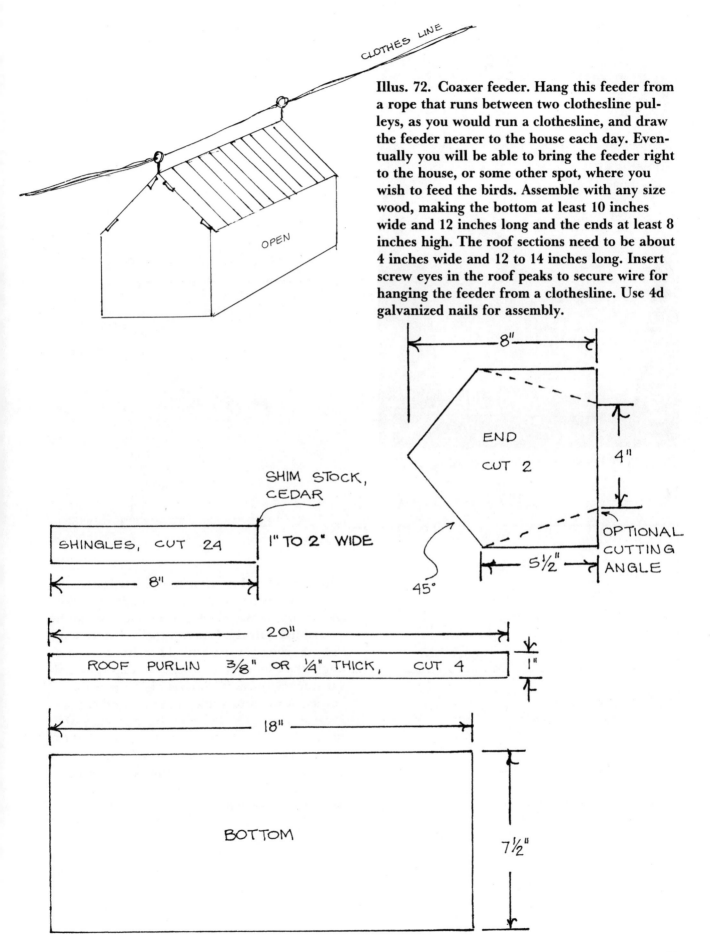

CLOTHES LINE

OPEN

Illus. 72. Coaxer feeder. Hang this feeder from a rope that runs between two clothesline pulleys, as you would run a clothesline, and draw the feeder nearer to the house each day. Eventually you will be able to bring the feeder right to the house, or some other spot, where you wish to feed the birds. Assemble with any size wood, making the bottom at least 10 inches wide and 12 inches long and the ends at least 8 inches high. The roof sections need to be about 4 inches wide and 12 to 14 inches long. Insert screw eyes in the roof peaks to secure wire for hanging the feeder from a clothesline. Use 4d galvanized nails for assembly.

8"

END
CUT 2

4"

OPTIONAL CUTTING ANGLE

45°

5½"

SHIM STOCK, CEDAR

SHINGLES, CUT 24

1" TO 2" WIDE

8"

20"

ROOF PURLIN 3/8" OR 1/4" THICK, CUT 4

1"

18"

BOTTOM

7½"

Illus. 73. Clear-view feeder, assembled.

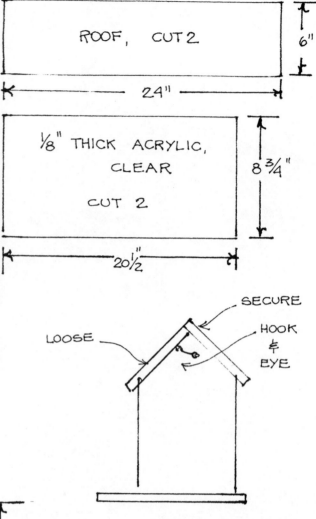

ROOF, CUT 2

6"

24"

⅛" THICK ACRYLIC, CLEAR CUT 2

8¾"

20½"

SECURE

LOOSE

HOOK & EYE

SIDE VIEW

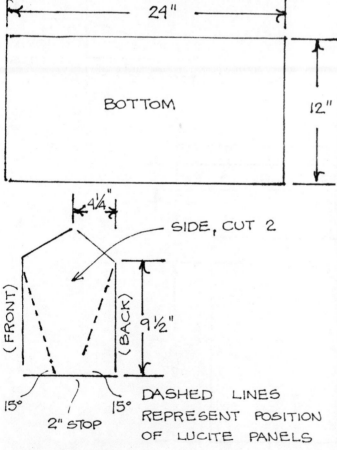

24"

BOTTOM

12"

4¼"

SIDE, CUT 2

(FRONT)

(BACK)

9½"

15°   15°

2" STOP

DASHED LINES REPRESENT POSITION OF LUCITE PANELS

Illus. 74. The clear-view feeder lets you know at a glance when feed is gone. Made of wafer board and ⅛-inch-thick acrylic sheet, it can be assembled quickly. Cut two roof sections and a bottom. Now cut two ends 12 inches high and angle the roof over 4¼ inches so that the vertical side measures 9½ inches high. From the corner of the roof angle, make a blind cut ½ inch deep at a 15° angle to the back edge of the feeder, all the way to the bottom. On the front edge, make the same sort of cut, but stop 2 inches from the bottom—this is the area where the feed slips out for the birds. Assemble sides to the bottom. Cut the acrylic sheets and slip them into place. (These are readily cut with a fine-toothed hand or power saw: I did these on a 60-tooth 10′ table saw blade.) Nail or screw the back roof section in place and install hook and eyes as shown to secure the front section. Refill the feeder through the opening made by removing this front section.

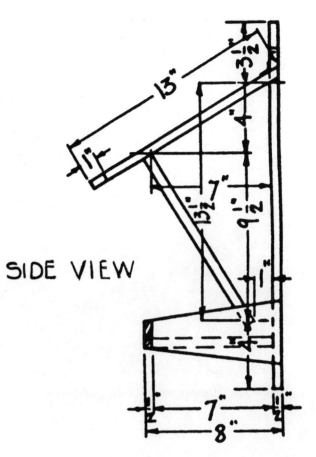

SIDE VIEW

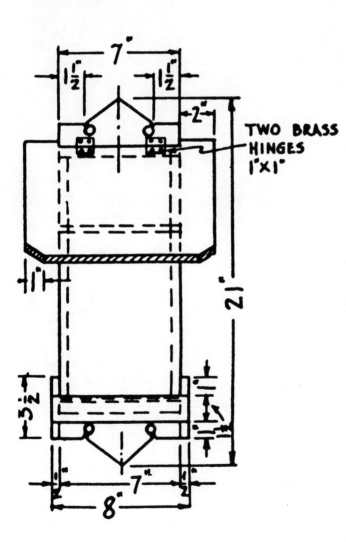

TWO BRASS
HINGES
1"X1"

FRONT VIEW

Illus. 75. Feeding boxes draw far more birds than nesting houses, and this version from Stanley Tools is fairly easy to build. Use ½-inch-thick redwood or cedar and 2d galvanized nails for assembly, making sure to drill pilot holes before nailing. Cut the back 7 inches wide and 21 inches long. The roof is 13 inches deep by 11 inches wide and requires two brass hinges to attach it to the back. The feeder holder at the bottom requires two pieces 3½ inches high tapering to 1 inch at the front (the taper is over the 7-inch depth of the pieces, which are attached to the sides of the back), with a 1″ × 8″ piece to prevent spillage. The feeder shelf is 7 inches square and fits inside the tapered pieces. Attach the feed holding box to the back and cut out the sides 13½ inches high, and cut the front 9½ inches long by 7 inches wide. Cut the sides of the feed holding box at a 45° angle at the front top edge, as shown, and a 30° angle at the back top edge. The overall width is 7 inches. Start assembly by attaching the feeding tray to the back, and then attach the feeder-box sides. Add the front and screw the hinges to the top and the back. The decorative cuts are optional.

Illus. 76. Boat-ended feeder, assembled.

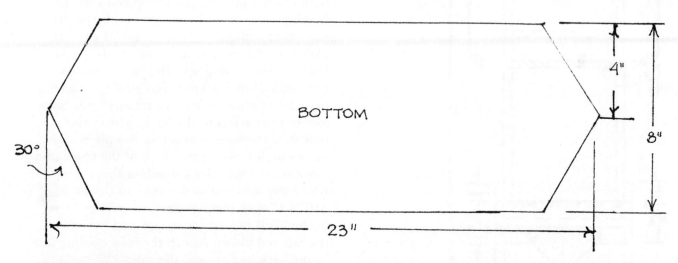

Illus. 77. This boat-ended feeder is my own design for greedy birds and severe weather. It is made of both redwood (the ends) and wafer board (top and bottom) and can be assembled quickly. Use ¾-inch-thick wafer board for the top and bottom. On the bottom, cut 15° angles at each end to provide a base for the boat ends. Make a 15° bevel on the top edges: this is most easily done with a table saw but can also be done, carefully, with a circular saw. Cut out the ends and attach them to the bottom, flush with the 15° ends and with the 15° angles meeting, using 4d galvanized nails or 1½-inch × No. 6 brass wood screws. Finally, install the top. If desired, quarter round or lattice moulding may be placed around the feeder edges to prevent spillage. Diagram continues on next page.

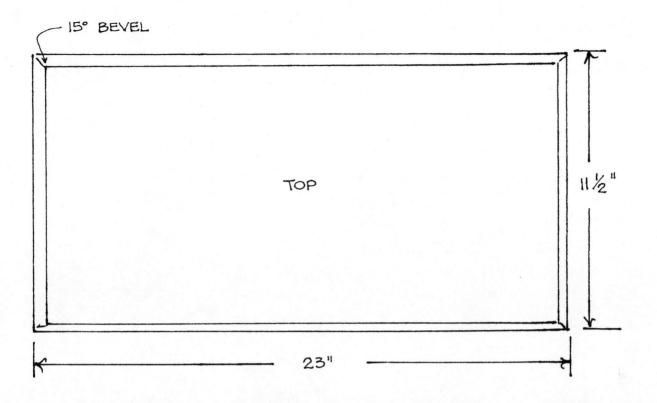

15° BEVEL

TOP

11½"

23"

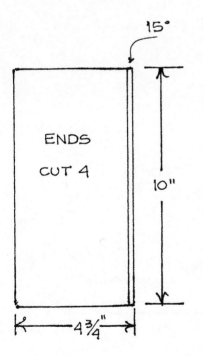

15°

ENDS
CUT 4

10"

4¾"

Illus. 77.

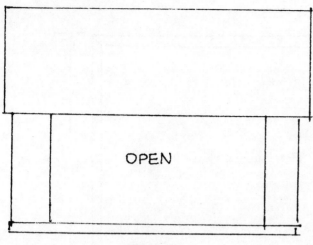

OPEN

FRONT

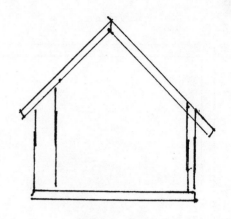

SIDE VIEW

¾" STOCK

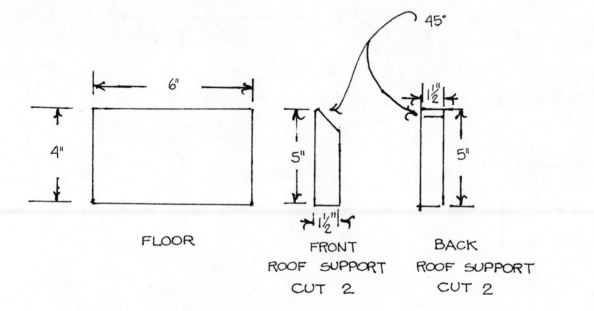

6"

4"

FLOOR

45°

5"

1½"

FRONT
ROOF SUPPORT
CUT 2

1½"

5"

BACK
ROOF SUPPORT
CUT 2

Illus. 78. Robin shelf. Use redwood and assemble with 1½-inch × No. 6 brass wood screws. Install the back roof supports and the back half of the roof, then check the angles on the front roof supports for correctness. If all is well, attach. If not, recut.

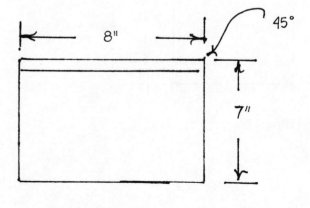

8"

45°

7"

ROOF
CUT 2

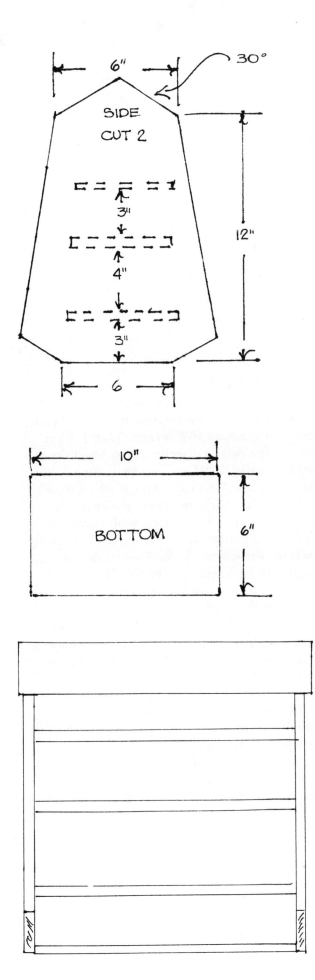

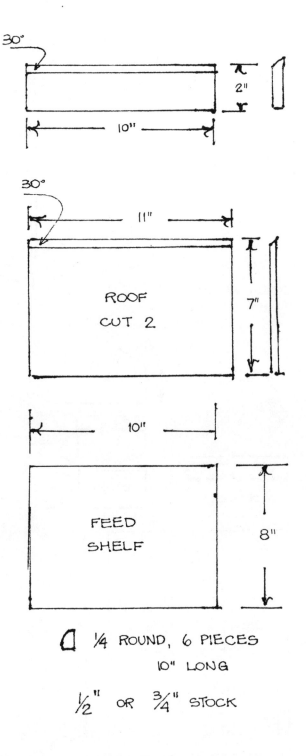

SIDE
CUT 2

6"

30°

3"

4"

3"

6

12"

BOTTOM

10"

6"

30°

2"

10"

30°

11"

ROOF
CUT 2

7"

10"

FEED
SHELF

8"

¼ ROUND, 6 PIECES
10" LONG

½" OR ¾" STOCK

Illus. 79. Four-level feeder of exterior-grade plywood. Assemble with 4d galvanized nails or 1½-inch × No. 6 brass wood screws. Attach the quarter round at the edges of the top three shelves to help keep feed in place.

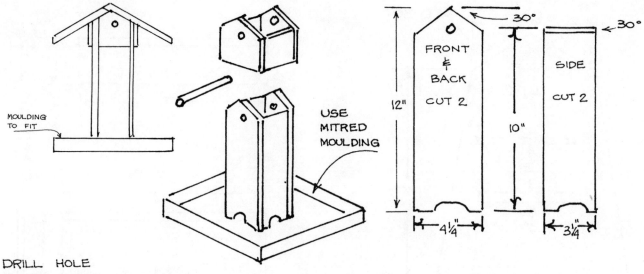

MOULDING TO FIT

USE MITRED MOULDING

FRONT & BACK CUT 2

12"

30°

SIDE CUT 2

30°

10"

4¼"

3¼"

DRILL HOLE TO FIT DOWEL

TOP PIECES

5¼"

30°

2½"

CUT 2

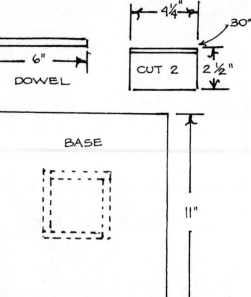

6"

DOWEL

4¼"

30°

CUT 2

2½"

BASE

11"

11"

12"

30°

ROOF

CUT 2

7"

Illus. 80. This lift-off-top feeder is for those who prefer more complex projects. Start by cutting out the redwood base (if necessary, the base can measure 10½ inches square). Then cut out the two roof sections and bevel the top edge on each at 30° angles. Next, cut out the sides and bevel the top edges at 30°. Cut out the front and back and bevel the edges that meet the roof at 30° angles. Drill holes one inch down and centered just larger than ⅜ inch for the dowel. At the base of sides and front and back, cut 2-inch-wide by 1½-inch-high arcs for the feed to run out onto the base. Now, cut the final top pieces. Start a 30° cut 2½ inches up each side and drill a slightly larger than ⅜-inch-diameter hole to match the spacing of those on the front and back. Cut out the other two top pieces and bevel the top edges at 30° angles. The last piece you'll need is a 6-inch-long by ⅜-inch-diameter dowel, which will fit more easily into the holes if one end is slightly pointed.

Start by assembling the sides, front and back, using 4d nails. Next, center this box on the base and attach with 1½-inch × No. 6 brass wood screws from underneath. Finally, assemble the lift-off-roof section, sides, front and back first, and then the roof, again using galvanized 4d finishing nails. If all has been cut properly, the roof section will readily slip over the base section, and the dowel will hold the roof in place. If you wish to add a finishing touch and diminish feed spillage, place mitred moulding around the outside edges of the base.

Illus. 81. A scrap-wood feeder sits well on top of a fence post. Add borders of quarter-round or other moulding to prevent excess spillage in windy areas.

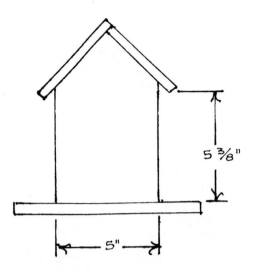

5 3⁄8"

5"

1" THICK STOCK

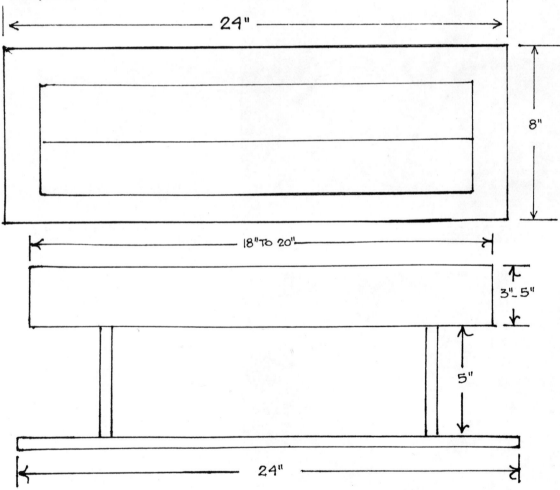

24"

8"

18"TO 20"

3"–5"

5"

24"

Illus. 82. Scrap-wood feeder. For a quick and easy feeder, this design by Don Geary is hard to beat. Don took a piece of slab wood, about 24″ × 8″, and routed out two ¾-inch-wide by ½-inch-deep grooves for the ends. The grooves are 5 inches long, about 4 inches in from each end of the slab wood, and centered. Into each of these, he placed an 8-inch-high end piece, with rounded sides, 5 inches wide, and he cut the top at 45° angles to accept the cedar shake roof. Only one shake is needed for each side of the roof.

Illus. 83. Scrap-wood feeder. Although similar to the one in Illus. 82, this feeder has a different roof.

Illus. 84. Installing roof strips for shingles.

Illus. 85. Attaching shingles.

Illus. 86. Use a heavy knife to trim shingles to the proper width on any bird house or feeder. Because shim stock varies greatly in width, exact dimensions are not possible and such trimming is often needed.

Illus. 87. Staining produces a barnlike look so that birds are more visually pleased than they might be with raw wood.

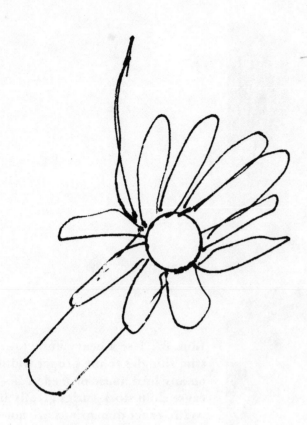

Illus. 88. This simple hummingbird feeder is nothing more than a small plastic or glass vial, with a plastic flower (bright colored) taped or cemented around its mouth. Wrap wire around the vial just behind the flower to hang it and make sure it is at a slight downward angle (as shown) when hung.

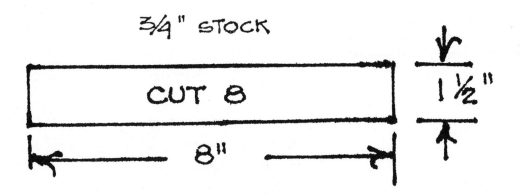

3/4" STOCK

CUT 8

8"

1 ½"

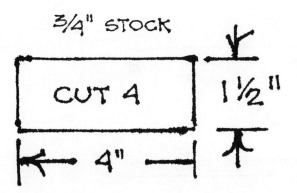

3/4" STOCK

CUT 4

4"

1 ½"

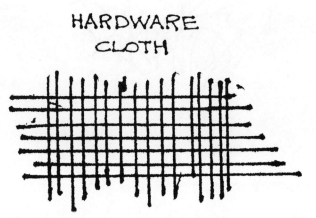

HARDWARE CLOTH

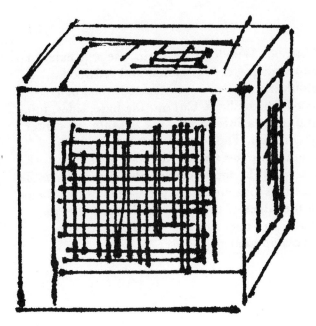

Illus. 89. Suet feeders are an integral part of winter feeding. And this one, made of redwood strips and hardware cloth, is easy to build. Attach one side with either hook and eyes or with wood screws (the hook and eyes are faster and last longer with frequent feedings). Staple the hardware cloth (galvanized metal, ¼-inch mesh) to the insides of the redwood strips.

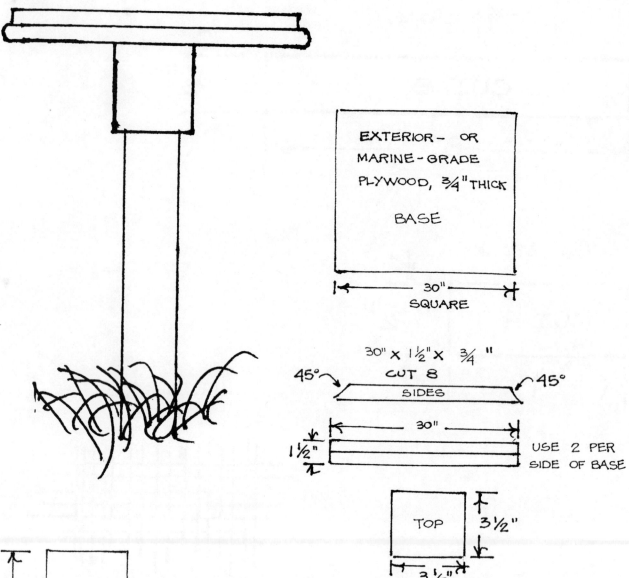

EXTERIOR – OR MARINE-GRADE PLYWOOD, ¾" THICK

BASE

30" SQUARE

30" X 1½" X ¾"
CUT 8
SIDES
45°   45°

1½"   30"

USE 2 PER SIDE OF BASE

TOP   3½"

3½"

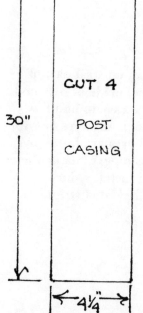

CUT 4

POST CASING

30"

4¼"

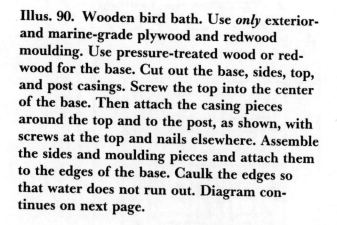

Illus. 90. Wooden bird bath. Use *only* exterior- and marine-grade plywood and redwood moulding. Use pressure-treated wood or redwood for the base. Cut out the base, sides, top, and post casings. Screw the top into the center of the base. Then attach the casing pieces around the top and to the post, as shown, with screws at the top and nails elsewhere. Assemble the sides and moulding pieces and attach them to the edges of the base. Caulk the edges so that water does not run out. Diagram continues on next page.

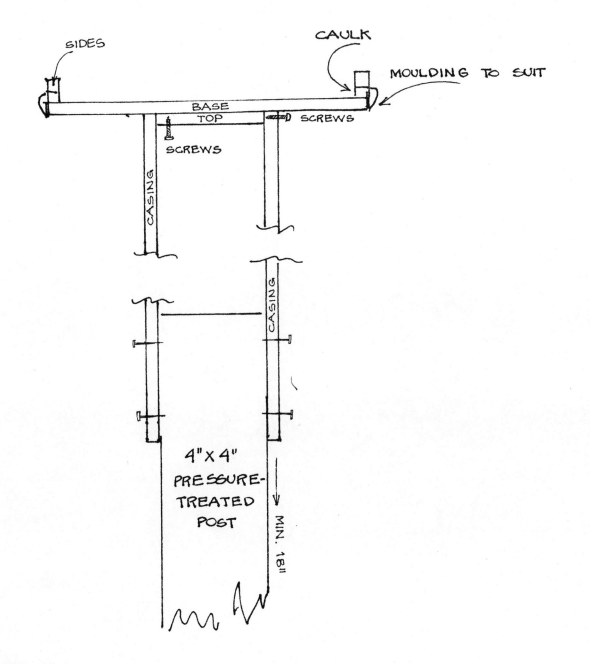

SIDES

CAULK

MOULDING TO SUIT

BASE
TOP

SCREWS

SCREWS

CASING

CASING

4" X 4"
PRESSURE-
TREATED
POST

MIN. 18"

Illus. 90.

9
BIRD FOODS

Bird Foods

As you can see, bird feeding is not limited to tossing a few sunflower seeds onto the ground to see which species will arrive. In fact, if you don't plan to continue the feeding throughout the winter then you shouldn't start a feeding program. Birds that depend on a feeding station and that might otherwise have migrated or gone elsewhere to feed may starve if their source is cut off in mid-winter. Year-round feeding is another story. If birds get used to feeding at your station (a group of feeders in one yard) during the year, many that would otherwise migrate or simply move to another local neighborhood may remain through the winter.

Populations vary throughout the year at feeding stations, though most stations seem to attract more birds in winter. This may be because the birds that remain feed more often when other food sources diminish during the cold months. Obviously during the spring growing seasons, when farmers' fields are full of seeds, the *need* for your feeding station decreases.

In any case, the odds are excellent that once begun, your feeding program has a good chance of expanding when winter arrives and in many areas well before. And if the kinds of birds you like to see are not visiting your yard at feeding time, you might reconsider the types and quantities of seed you're putting out. Aggressive species will take over if there is overcrowding, which alone may force you to provide more feeders if you wish to see birds other than starlings and evening grosbeaks.

Single Feeding Stations

Single feeding stations (several feeders that contain one kind of food) are easy to supply, but some birds fight others for the seed. Chickadees get along with other birds, except raptors, but sparrows and starlings are more aggressive. Birds that are less pushy are quickly shoved off the feeding line, so it's helpful to know which foods certain birds prefer, how to serve it, and where. Then you can reduce the undesirable species around your feeder; you'll almost certainly never eliminate them.

Ground Feeders

When I lived in upstate New York, a single towhee would slip into the feeding line. No matter how many evening grosbeaks arrived, the towhee ignored all other birds and pecked away at the spillage. For some reason, that was the only towhee I was able to attract to that feeder, and he, like many other birds, definitely preferred feeding from the ground. In the five years of observing him, I don't remember that bird ever getting on the feeder, assuming it was the same towhee all the time.

Other ground feeders include juncos, sparrows, doves (most of which are pigeons), cardinals, jays, thrashers, starlings, and flickers.

Although I've never seen a flicker eat from a feeding platform, they are not listed as ground feeders in my reference books on feeding.

Most other birds will feed from feeders, though swinging feeders don't seem to attract many jays or sparrows. Cardinals, however, seem to like such feeders, as do chickadees, nuthatches, and a few others.

Foods

Many types of mixed and single bird seeds are available. If you live in or near a rural area or in a suburban area where horses are kept, the best place to buy feed is at a feed and grain dealer. Don't buy in small quantities. Look for the 25- or 50-pound or larger sacks of feed for horses and cows. Buying in bulk saves money, and the price of grain in such stores tends to be somewhat lower than elsewhere. Some people in rural and suburban areas still buy from the garden department at a large store where prices may be 200 percent higher.

In my area, I have located a farm supplier where I can trim 25 percent off the bill. The price is lower because the supplier grinds and cracks his own feed, while other places serve as retail outlets for several brands.

Sunflower seed. This type of feed is extraordinarily expensive and is sometimes fed separately, but it's eaten so quickly (most birds like it) that it's far cheaper to buy in at least 50-pound bags. In previous years, I have used as much as 25 pounds of sunflower seed in a single *week*.

Kernels alone are available, but the cost goes up tremendously, and since I've never fed it, I don't know the rate at which it would be used. You'll find that even tiny birds, like chickadees and nuthatches, are willing to work for their supper—cracking their own sunflower seeds to get the kernels inside. In fact, if you're having difficulty with starlings or sparrows, you might discourage their visits by stocking sunflower seeds. They have some difficulty cracking the seed cases. One of my problems with grosbeaks, however, was controlling their voracious appetite for sunflower seeds.

Rake and discard the sunflower seed cases in spring. Don't feed them to your garden. For some reason, the material in sunflower seed cases harms, rather than helps, plant growth.

Corn. Be sure to buy corn at a feed supplier rather than at your local pet shop or in a garden department. I've never noted a price difference of less than 75 percent. It's usually over 100 percent and sometimes as much as 250 percent. Again, figure on buying at least a 25-pound bag. You can save even more on larger bags.

You should crack the corn before serving it to the birds. Place it in the feeder in dry weather or when your feeding station is very busy, because it tends to spoil rapidly once it is wetted down even in cold weather. If you do serve the corn in wet weather, be sure to remove the leftovers to prevent the birds from getting sick.

Select a grade of mixed feeds, known as scratch feed. It is usually fed to chickens, which are always scratching at the ground for feed even when the feed is elsewhere. Choose fine, medium, or coarse scratch feed according to the size birds you're trying hardest to attract. Scratch feed is even less expensive than the other feeds mentioned.

Thistle. Although included in many premixed birdseeds, thistle can also be bought separately. Although it's bulky, the price per pound is very high, so you'll probably want to limit its use and place it in special feeders when serving with no other seed. This keeps it from being totally wiped off of the board either by overly enthusiastic birds or by winds. Since it doesn't suffer from wet weather, thistle is an appropriate feed for spring and fall—before it's really cold enough to serve other feeds. Thistle tends to increase the arrival of chickadees, juncos, titmice, and, less fortunately, sparrows.

Mixed wild bird foods. These bird foods fluctuate widely in cost, depending on the ingredients in the mixture. You might find a reasonably priced small bag in your local garden shop or supermarket as an enticement, but if possible check around at feed suppliers. In most cases, you'll find it makes far more sense to make your own mix with ingredients that will attract the bird species you want. Some ingredients are hard to locate and expensive even in bulk form. Most people usually start with perhaps 25 pounds of the fancy wild bird food mix. After the birds have exhausted this supply, feed them sunflower seeds, cracked corn, millet, suet, and other delicacies separately. Don't mix them with one another.

Suet. Suet is fat that has been trimmed from beef and mutton. Supermarkets usually package it in the winter. You might have a hard time locating it in warm weather. Because it spoils quickly under a warm sun and because birds don't need the extra nourishment in warm weather, suet should be fed to birds only in winter.

Today, suet is expensive in most communities. If you live in a rural area where people still slaughter their own beef or if you raise your own, you should have no problem obtaining suet. In most areas, large meat packers are no longer getting "all but the squeal" from hogs, but they are getting just about everything except the swish of a cow's tail from beef animals.

Food Desirability

The kind of birds you draw to your feeding stations during cold weather depends a great deal on the kind of seed you supply. During warm weather and particularly in late spring and early summer, the birds' need for, and reaction to, well-filled feeding stations drops. Breads, for instance, and many baked products are cheap and easy to supply but seem to be less desirable as nutritional aids, because they are metabolized rapidly. To the basic grain-suet diet, you can add anything from peanut butter (mix it with suet to reduce the cost), to the whole peanut, to your leftover popcorn from last night's movie.

Since birds do not have teeth and can't chew or grind food as humans do, their diet must include a substance that will grind the food in their stomach. Grit is the usual addition to feed. To keep up calcium levels, many chicken feeders add crunched sea shells to their birds' diets. Both are available from a farm feed shop. Coarse sand or even coal ash, if nothing else can be found, can also be used.

All sorts of moderate-to-expensive foods, including fruits and berries, are pleasing to birds. You have a wide array of choices around which your flock can gather. The list below will give a general idea of which birds favor which foods.

Foods	Birds
Cracked corn	Several woodpeckers and most songbirds, including sparrows, blackbirds, grackles.
Breads, cakes	Just about every nonraptor.
Sunflower seed	Cardinals, finches, sparrows, juncos, cowbirds, chickadees, most other songbirds, many other birds as well.
Suet	Almost all birds during cold weather.
Oats	Black-capped chickadees seem particularly fond of oats.
Mixed seed	Many if not all songbirds, most other birds.
Thistle	Finches, sparrows, chickadees, towhees, juncos, doves.

If you want to specialize your feeding to attract particular birds, I suggest spending a day at your public library. Several books list foods preferred by many, many types of birds. Some feeds tend towards the exotic. They are difficult to prepare or very expensive, and none is very practical. But some people don't mind spending time preparing and cooking for birds.

Appendixes

Appendix A

Wood Suitability

Species	Locale	Characteristics & Uses
Ash	East of Rockies	Strong and heavy, with a tough, close, straight grain that takes a fine finish; ideal for making durable birdhouses.
Basswood	Eastern half of U.S., but not near coasts	Used mainly for low-grade furniture, basswood offers good workability but requires a durable finish.
Birch	East of Mississippi, southeastern Canada	Hard and durable, most birch is acceptable for making bird structures but does not withstand weathering well. Takes paint very well.
Butternut	Southern Canada, Minnesota, eastern U.S. to Alabama and Florida	A walnut-colored soft hardwood, though not as soft as basswood; easily worked, reasonably strong, with coarse grain; does not withstand weathering well.
Cypress	Maryland to Texas and along the Mississippi Valley to Indiana	Resembles white cedar, is water-resistant, very durable, usually expensive, and difficult to find.
Douglas fir	Pacific Coast and British Columbia	Strong, light, and clear-grained; tends to be brittle, but the heartwood is somewhat resistant to effects of weathering; readily available in most areas and moderately priced.
Hickory	Common from southern Virginia to New York, Ohio, Tennessee, and Kentucky	A very heavy, hard, and tough wood; tends to check and shrink; is hard to work and doesn't resist insects or decay well; easy to locate in much of the East, but nearly impossible to find in the West; expensive and difficult to use for making bird structures; use only if you have it on hand.
Live oak	Common along the coasts of Oregon, California, and the southern Atlantic and Gulf states	Heavy, hard, tough, strong, and durable; hard to work, but otherwise nearly perfect for most bird structures.
Maple	All states east of Colorado; southern Canada	Heavy, tough, strong, fairly easy to work but not durable, although a fine wood for birdhouses; may be expensive because it's hard to find in certain areas; different varieties offer different properties; rock, or sugar, maple is the hardest and most popular.
Norway pine	States bordering the Great Lakes	Light-colored, moderately hard softwood; not durable; fairly easy to work.
Poplar	Virginia, West Virginia, Tennessee, Kentucky, and along the Mississippi Valley	Soft, cheap hardwood; easily obtainable in wide boards because of rapid, straight tree growth; rots quickly if not protected but works easily and is finely textured.

Species	Locale	Characteristics & Uses
Red cedar	East of Colorado and north of Florida	Very, very light, soft, weak, and brittle wood with great durability, works easily; is hard to find and costly in wide-board form; excellent for birdhouses.
Red oak	Virginia, West Virginia, Tennessee, Arkansas, Kentucky, Ohio, Missouri, Maryland, and parts of New York	A coarse-grained, easily warped wood that doesn't last long; avoid outdoor uses.
Redwood	California	Ideal for birdhouses but expensive; not as strong as yellow pine; shrinks and splits only a little; is straight-grained and exceptionally durable without any finish; many inexpensive grades are available.
Spruce	New York, New England, West Virginia, the Great Lakes states, Idaho, Washington, Oregon, and through much of central Canada	A light, soft, fairly durable wood with close grain; makes good bird structures.
White cedar	Eastern coast of the United States and around the Great Lakes	A soft, light, close-grained wood, exceedingly durable and nearly ideal for birdhouses.
White oak	Virginia, West Virginia, Tennessee, Arkansas, Kentucky, Ohio, Missouri, Maryland, and Indiana	Heavy, hard, strong, with a moderately coarse-grain pattern; tough and dense; the most durable of all North American native hardwoods, fairly easy to work except for a tendency to check and shrink; may be expensive in some areas.
White pine	Minnesota, Wisconsin, Maine, Michigan, Idaho, Montana, Washington, Oregon, California, and in stands in some eastern states other than Maine	A fine-grained, easily worked wood that can sometimes be found with few knots; durable, soft, but not very strong, more than suitable for birdhouses; economical in most communities.
Yellow pine	Virginia to Texas; several species are classified as southern pine, which are somewhat knottier and harder to work than white pine	Hard, tough softwood; heartwood is durable with the grain; hard to nail; saws easily; an inexpensive and excellent wood for bird structures.

Approximate Number of Wire Nails per Pound (Theoretical Average)

Steel Wire Gauge	LENGTH — INCHES																					
	3/16	1/4	3/8	1/2	5/8	3/4	7/8	1	1 1/8	1 1/4	1 1/2	1 3/4	2	2 1/4	2 1/2	2 3/4	3	3 1/2	4	4 1/2	5	6
2								60	54	48	41	35	31	28	25	23	21	18	16	14	13	11
3								67	60	55	47	41	36	32	29	27	25	21	18	16	15	12
4								81	74	66	55	48	41	37	34	31	29	25	22	20	18	15
5								90	81	74	61	52	45	41	38	35	32	28	24	22	21	
6				213	174	149	128	113	101	91	76	65	58	52	47	43	39	34	29	26	24	20
7				250	205	174	148	132	120	110	92	78	70	61	55	53	51	40	35	31	28	24
8				272	238	198	174	153	139	126	106	93	82	74	66	61	56	48	42	38	34	28
9				348	286	238	213	185	170	152	128	112	99	87	79	71	67	58	50	45	44	34
10				469	373	320	277	242	216	196	165	142	124	111	100	91	84	71	62	55	49	42
11				510	417	366	323	285	254	233	200	171	149	136	122	111	103	87	77	69	61	52
12				740	603	511	442	405	351	327	268	229	204	182	161	149	137	118	103	95	87	71
13			1356	1017	802	688	590	508	458	412	348	294	260	232	209	175	153	138	123	110	93	
14		2293	1664	1290	1037	863	806	667	610	536	459	406	350	312	278	233	201	176	157	140	117	
15		2890	2213	1619	1316	1132	971	869	787	694	578	501	437	390	351	317	290	246	220	196	177	145
16		3932	2720	2142	1708	1414	1229	1090	973	872	739	635	553	496	452	410	370	318	277	248	226	
17		5316	3890	2700	2303	1904	1581	1409	1253	1139	956	831	746	666	590	532	486	418	360	322	295	
18		7520	5072	3824	3130	2608	2248	1976	1760	1590	1338	1150	996	890	820	740	680	585	507			
19		9920	6860	5075	4132	3508	2816	2556	2284	2096	1772	1590	1390	1205	1060	970	895	800				
20	18620	14050	9432	7164	5686	4795	4230	3596	3225	2893	2412	2070	1810	1620	1450	1315	1215	1435				

Penny Size Conversion Chart

Nail length is often designated by penny (d) size. The letter "d" is the English symbol for pound. It also means penny in the English monetary system. The theory is that penny size represented the number of pounds a thousand nails weighed. Today this antiquated system represents only the length of nails. It does **NOT** indicate count per pound, diameter, style and size head, or other characteristics.

PENNY SIZE	2d	3d	4d	5d	6d	7d	8d	9d	10d	12d
LENGTH — INCHES	1"	1¼"	1½"	1¾"	2"	2¼"	2½"	2¾"	3"	3¼"

PENNY SIZE	16d	20d	30d	40d	50d	60d	70d	80d	90d	100d
LENGTH — INCHES	3½"	4"	4½"	5"	5½"	6"	7"	8"	9"	10"

Color-Coded Blister Pak Nails

STOCK NUMBER	PIECES	COLOR CODE	DESCRIPTION
HMC-000	30	Yellow	★ ¾" Concrete Screw Nails - Helyx™
HMC-010	24	Yellow	★ 1" Concrete Screw Nails - Helyx™
HMC-020	18	Yellow	★ 1½" Concrete Screw Nails - Helyx™
HMC-030	14	Yellow	★ 2" Concrete Screw Nails - Helyx™
HMC-040	12	Yellow	★ 2½" Concrete Screw Nails - Helyx™
HMC-050	10	Yellow	★ 3" Concrete Screw Nails - Helyx™
HMC-100	30	Blue	★ ¾" Masonry Nails
HMC-110	24	Blue	★ 1" Masonry Nails
HMC-120	16	Blue	★ 1½" Masonry Nails
HMC-130	14	Blue	★ 2" Masonry Nails
HMC-140	12	Blue	★ 2½" Masonry Nails
HMC-150	10	Blue	★ 3" Masonry Nails
HMC-200	12	Pink	★ 8D (2½") Furring Nails - Hard Cut
HMC-300	44	Purple	1¾" x .083 Wood Siding Nails - Ring-Barb™, Electro-Galvanized
HMC-400	40	Orange	1¼" x .083 Underlay Nails - Ring-Barb™
HMC-500	20	Red	2" x No. 5 Underlay Screw Nails - Helyx™
HMC-600	16	Aqua	2½" x No. 6 Drive Screw Nails - Helyx™
HMC-700	26	Olive Green	1⅜" x .105 Drywall Nails - Ring-Barb™
HMC-800	20	Green	2½" x No. 5 Flooring Screw Nails - Helyx™
HMC-900	20	Tan	2½" x .115 Flooring Nails - Rol-Thread™, Hard

Made by Hillwood Manufacturing Co. and available from local hardware dealers.

Appendix C

Birdhouse Size Requirements

Types	Floor Size in Inches	Entry-Hole Size in Inches	Hole above Floor in Inches	Interior Depth in Inches	Nest above Ground in Feet
Bluebirds Eastern and Western	5 × 5	1½	6	8	5–10
Chickadees black-capped, Carolina, gray-headed Boreal & chestnut-backed	4 × 4	1⅛	6–8	8–10	6–15
Finch house	6 × 6	2	4	6	8–12
Flycatchers great-crested, olivaceous, Western	6 × 6	2	6–8	8–10	8–20
Nuthatches white-breasted, red-breasted	4 × 4	1¼	6–8	8–10	5–20
brown-headed	2 × 3	1	6–8	8–10	5–20
Owls barn	10 × 18	6	4	15–18	12–18
screech	8 × 8	3	9–12	12–15	10–30
barred	13 × 15	8	—	16	10–30
Phoebes Eastern and black	6 × 6	open, one side	—	6	8–12
Sparrows song	6 × 6	open, all sides	—	6	1–3
house	4 × 4	1½	6–8	8–10	4–12
Swallows barn		open, one side	—	6	8–12
purple martin	6 × 6	2½	1	6	15–20
tree	5 × 5	1½	1–5	6	10–15
Thrushes (American robin)	6 × 8	open, one side	—	8	6–15
Titmice plain, tufted, and bridled	4 × 4	1¼	6–8	8–10	6–15
Warbler prothonary	4 × 4	1½	5	8	4–7

Types	Floor Size in Inches	Entry-Hole Size in Inches	Hole above Floor in Inches	Interior Depth in Inches	Nest above Ground in Feet
Woodpeckers					
downy	4 × 4	1¼	6–8	8–10	6–20
flicker	7 × 7	2½	14–16	16–18	6–20
hairy	6 × 6	1½	9–12	12–15	12–20
redheaded	6 × 6	2	9–12	12–15	12–20
pileated	8 × 8	3–4	10–12	12–30	12–60
red-bellied	6 × 6	2½	10–12	12–14	12–20
Wrens					
brown-throated	4 × 4	1	1–6	6–8	6–10
Carolina	4 × 4	1⅛	1–6	6–8	6–10
house	4 × 4	1	1–6	6–8	6–10
winter	4 × 4	1 × 2½	4–6	6–8	5–10

As you can see, not a great deal of wood is required for any birdhouse. The exceptions are houses for woodpeckers and owls. Even birdhouses that are larger than usual require a small amount of wood.

Note, too, that as little as one foot in hanging height can make a big difference in the birds you attract. If you desire winter wrens, for instance, one less foot in height will help keep out other wrens.

Make certain that all entry holes 1½ inches and smaller in diameter are sized exactly in order to keep starlings out.

Appendix D

Metric Conversion Chart

UNIT	ABBREVIATION	APPROXIMATE U.S. EQUIVALENT			
Length					
		Number of Metres			
myriametre	mym	10,000	———— 6.2 miles		
kilometre	km	1000	0.62 mile		
hectometre	hm	100	109.36 yards		
dekametre	dam	10	32.81 feet		
metre	m	1	39.37 inches		
decimetre	dm	0.1	3.94 inches		
centimetre	cm	0.01	0.39 inch		
millimetre	mm	0.001	0.04 inch		
Area					
		Number of Square Metres			
square kilometre	sq km *or* km²	1,000,000	0.3861 square miles		
hectare	ha	10,000	2.47 acres		
are	a	100	119.60 square yards		
centare	ca	1	10.76 square feet		
square centimetre	sq cm *or* cm²	0.0001	0.155 square inch		
Volume					
		Number of Cubic Metres			
dekastere	das	10	13.10 cubic yards		
stere	s	1	1.31 cubic yards		
decistere	ds	0.10	3.53 cubic feet		
cubic centimetre	cu cm *or* cm³ *also* cc	0.000001	0.061 cubic inch		
Capacity					
		Number of Litres	*Cubic*	*Dry*	*Liquid*
kilolitre	kl	1000	1.31 cubic yards		
hectolitre	hl	100	3.53 cubic feet	2.84 bushels	
dekalitre	dal	10	0.35 cubic foot	1.14 pecks	2.64 gallons
litre	l	1	61.02 cubic inches	0.908 quart	1.057 quarts
decilitre	dl	0.10	6.1 cubic inches	0.18 pint	0.21 pint
centilitre	cl	0.01	0.6 cubic inch		0.338 fluidounce
millilitre	ml	0.001	0.06 cubic inch		0.27 fluidram
Mass and Weight					
		Number of Grams			
metric ton	MT *or* t	1,000,000	1.1 tons		
quintal	q	100,000	220.46 pounds		
kilogram	kg	1,000	2.2046 pounds		
hectogram	hg	100	3.527 ounces		
dekagram	dag	10	0.353 ounce		
gram	g *or* gm	1	0.035 ounce		
decigram	dg	0.10	1.543 grains		
centigram	cg	0.01	0.154 grain		
milligram	mg	0.001	0.015 grain		

American Term	British Term
rabbet	rebate
finishing nail	lost head nail
flathead screw	countersink screw
screw eye	wood screw with ringed shank

Index

Numbers in italic refer to pages with illustrations.